T0154008

Massage Therapist Success Mindset

MASSAGE THERAPIST
SUCCESS
MINDSET

SUCCESS PRINCIPLES FOR THE MASSAGE THERAPIST ENTREPRENEUR

RICHARD J. PLATT

NEW YORK

LONDON • NASHVILLE • MELBOURNE • VANCOUVER

Massage Therapist Success Mindset

Success Principles for the Massage Therapist Entrepreneur

© 2021 Richard J. Platt

Published in New York, New York, by Morgan James Publishing. Morgan James is a trademark of Morgan James, LLC. www.MorganJamesPublishing.com

ISBN 9781642798715 paperback
ISBN 9781642798722 eBook
Library of Congress Control Number: 2020930288

Cover & Interior Design by:
Christopher Kirk
www.GFSstudio.com

Morgan James is a proud partner of Habitat for Humanity Peninsula and Greater Williamsburg. Partners in building since 2006.

Get involved today! Visit
MorganJamesPublishing.com/giving-back

Dedication

To my Mother, Brenda, whose unwavering support and love has carried me through some of the toughest times of my life. You are the kindest, most creative and talented person I know. Thank you for being my biggest fan, my confidante, and my best friend. I love you.

Acknowledgements

It's important to me that I recognize the people who have made the biggest impact on the creation of this book, and the unwavering support of the ones I have within my experience.

From the time I was a child, I had always dreamt about being an entrepreneur and business owner. Even though I had to go through all the life events that were needed for me to grow into who I am today, I couldn't have done it without some of the most pinnacle events and influential people that have come into my life experience.

First and foremost, I thank my best friend and kindred spirit Amanda C., who is my very own personal mastermind and accountability partner. Amanda and I have been inseparable best friends since the young and impressionable age of 16. Amanda, you have shown me the meaning of unconditional love and true friendship.

My parents, John and Brenda, who created a safe space for me to go in times of my life when I felt I needed to recharge and escape. As a child, you sometimes forget the sacrifices your parents make for you so that you can be successful in whatever you set out to do.

My supportive and loving partner Sandy, who shows me the art of kindness and compassion every single day. I hope that I can one day embody even a fraction of the type of person you are to everyone you encounter. Your patience and acceptance of everyone is the perfect image of what I strive to become, which takes most people lifetimes. My world is a much better place because I've been blessed to have you in it.

My late Gran Betty, who raised my mother and whose spiritual nature inspired me to pull back the veil and to see the hidden meaning behind life. My Gran showed me that there are forces in this world and universe that our human brains might not ever comprehend, but they are there, and they are directing and guiding us whether we believe in them or not.

My mentor Bob Proctor, who taught me so much through his straightforward, no bull approach to solving perceived problems we have, through his reminders that we create our own reality. I have thoroughly enjoyed being in your company on our training visits in Toronto, Ontario, and and I am grateful for all the mentorship and direction you have given me.

Finally, the events around my very first massage therapy position contained the launching platform which ultimately ended up being the basis of why I wrote this book. That experience caused me to want to help other practitioners who are in a position where they want to start their own practice but might have self-doubt and fear that prevents them from moving forward with it. When the owners of that practice let me go and tried to place fear and doubt in my mind around opening my own business, they sparked my burning desire to prove to myself that I could indeed do it and be successful.

I have you both to thank most of all.

Table of Contents

Introduction

"Understanding your old belief system and the limitations it places on you, puts you back into the driver's seat. You now become the programmer to the program and turn off the auto pilot switch on what no longer propels you forward into the career you want to have, and the life you want to live."
Richard J. Platt

Success Principles for the Massage Therapist Entrepreneur

I have no doubt in my mind that each one of you can employ the principles discussed in this book to work for you in wonderful ways that will propel you into the career you're meant to have, and the life you're meant to live.

Each day, I study these principles and others, so that I live my own life to the fullest and help those I meet who might need my help. One of the best feelings in the world for me is seeing someone begin to make massive leaps in their awareness and then their results.

It's very easy to slip into your old way of thinking and your old way of doing things. By interrupting those thought patterns and changing your routines with the information in this book, you will notice subtle, yet powerful shifts in your awareness and thus your results. However, like anything you do that you want to develop, you must practice every day or else you will very easily slide back into old routines and old results.

You will not be the same person that you are now when you reach your goals. If you were, you wouldn't be reading this book. I'm here to raise your awareness and expand your consciousness to new ideas that I know if practiced, will take you from just working in an industry of helping people, to creating a fulfilling and abundant career that will allow you to carve your journey into whatever it is you truly want it to be.

Richard

"You know that without a doubt, you can be doing something you love, earning more while working less if you trusted that image in your mind. But then you sabotage it with fear of the unknown."

CHAPTER 1

The Struggle is Real

Why is it that so many massage therapists fail at entrepreneurship before they even start?

How is it possible that someone with fantastic education in a specific field, can be held hostage in their career because they don't know how to move forward with something more meaningful?

Do you wake up each morning knowing that you must go to a place to work where you're not happy? Do you feel that your work doesn't fulfill you in a way that you would like? Or the way you had hoped? This is by far one of the most unsatisfying emotions that someone can feel in their career.

Too often this happens to massage therapists, and too often the ones who are experiencing this do nothing about it. Sure, you can always get a better paying job at a different clinic, spa or center. You're more than qualified, you're good at what you do, and you genuinely enjoy helping and healing people; that's why you're in your massage therapy profession in the first place.

But something is missing. You want more. This wanting usually comes from knowing that you don't have the power or control to make big decisions within your place of employment or even your career in general while you're working under someone else.

To make matters worse, you don't control a large amount of the income you bring into that business. On average, most massage therapists give up around 50% of their client earnings and hand it right over to the business they are working for. If you work for a spa, that's even lower!! Most spa massage therapists are fully qualified to work in a focused therapeutic setting, but instead feel as though where they are currently is stable for the most part and is guaranteed income. I was chatting to a massage therapist the other day who worked at a spa where she has been for a few years and she only makes 30% of her earnings. THIRTY PERCENT! This massage therapist had 4000 hours of education under her belt along with a bunch of other complementary modalities, but she chooses to work for 30% and to top it off, she sometimes works 12-hour days.

CONFIDENCE BLOCK

When I asked this particular massage therapist if she ever considered opening up her own practice and having people work for HER instead, her reply was something that I hear so often and even felt myself, "I would love to, but I'm too scared that I will fail, and I feel like I don't know what I'm doing." So, because of this limiting belief, she stays locked into the routine of what she knows she can accomplish, within the safety net of her current employer.

I know you can relate to her; we all can! You love your job and even the people you work with, well, most of them anyways. But you want something more. You want to be able to have that full autonomy where you can dip into your creative ideas of how you would run your own massage therapy business, earn more money and have other therapists paying YOU to work out of YOUR space. You want to build your own dream and not someone else's.

There is just one problem, the "how." How can you create this type of business? You may have some existing debt; you're not making all that much money from working where you currently are at so saving is tough. Then there is the problem of not having any experience in running your own business. Then WHAM… dream crushed, too much risk and not enough direction so you stay stuck exactly where you are like so many other massage therapists do.

JUST IMAGINE FOR A MINUTE

But, just imagine for a second and entertain that thought that you fast forward a year or two into the future. You picture yourself being exactly where you want to be. You took the leap and you decided that you were going to go for it. You decided to believe in yourself and start your own business. In this image, you have your business and everything around you is set up EXACTLY how YOU want it. You look through your online scheduler and you see that business is good! You have clients on waiting lists to get into your business. Maybe you have a reception staff, other massage therapists working on clients out of your place of business and happily paying YOU so they can do so. Your business is thriving, and you are continually growing it, bettering it and feeling fulfilled in what you do. The best part for you is that you have a massive amount of passive income coming in from the services you offer. You want to take off for a couple weeks? Done! You still have money coming into your well-oiled business machine.

Now just think, if you saw that image inside your mind and it excited you and scared you at the same time, fantastic! Even if it wasn't that exact image, but something equally as rewarding for you within your career, also fantastic! You know that without a doubt, you can be doing something you love, earning more while working less if you trusted that image in your mind. But then you sabotage it with fear of the unknown, fear of not knowing how you're going to get there.

Some of the greatest, most successful entrepreneurs had very little money and very little idea of how they were going to accomplish building their business empire, or even where to start. But what they did have was the vision in their mind of what they wanted and the desire to keep moving towards it.

I UNDERSTAND

I know where you are at right now with all of this because I was there too. For me though, the excitement of having the decision-making power to do what I felt was best for my business was enough to keep me thinking about what I wanted. Like you, I wanted my very own space to work out of where

ALL the money I earned went back into my dream and my business, not someone else's. I wanted someone paying ME to work out of MY clinic.

I figured out how to move through those self-defeating thoughts of not being able to do it, not being smart enough, not having enough money and that fear of embarrassing myself through public failure. Through this process, I learned how to accomplish any goal I set out to reach. I became happier and more fulfilled. I earned more money and because I was now at a place where I wanted to be within my career, my personal life improved dramatically as well. My health was much better, my relationships were more meaningful, and I had more time for the things that really mattered in my life.

Throughout this book, you are going to find a lot of fantastic, mind-expanding information that I coach my clients through. This information is going to help you understand that through your own self-image and beliefs, you will be able to create something for yourself that you previously didn't think was possible.

I did.

"THE FOCUS I HAD ON MY
UNHAPPINESS WAS KEEPING
ME IN THE SAME SPOT
AND RESTRICTING ME
FROM FREEDOM."

CHAPTER 2

My Story

How I decided on my own goal, with the help of getting fired.

I worked hard for my massage therapy certification. There was a lot of studying anatomy and physiology, alongside medical intake knowledge and the understanding of contraindications that come along with any sort of massage therapy treatments. I knew that I was working towards a certification that would dramatically improve my own life and open many doors for me, and that was enough to keep me dedicated to the study and art of learning massage.

When it came time to graduate, like many other new massage therapists, I leapt at the first opportunity that came my way to work out of a space with other qualified massage therapists and complimentary practitioners/modalities. I didn't know a whole lot about negotiation of wages, or even the types of clients I wanted to work on as I was still getting my feet wet in this new industry. I do remember though, that my first ever paying client was a 7-month pregnant lady whom I had to perform side lying technique on. I was terrified that I was going to kill her baby, or even worse, both her and her baby! Now obviously my fear came from my own lack of skill and experience, but I was quickly forced to step through that fear and give the best massage I could at the time. The baby did not die, and the mother survived as well, so even though my fears were very real in my mind, the outcome was a very different experience.

THE JOURNEY

For over a year, I worked out of a small clinic in my hometown of about 20,000 people at the time. The clinic was run by two individuals who were both experienced massage therapists and who clearly had a dream and goal of creating something larger. I rented a room which was based on client percentage split of 50%, that had no cap on it. This meant that I paid 50% of my earnings to the clinic so I could operate out of their space, and if I had a good month, then I would still have to give half of that to the clinic. I was happy that I was able to be working out of somewhere, but there was this feeling after awhile of being restricted on what I could do and how much I could earn. I felt like I was trying to run through molasses.

After several months, I started to get restless with the sense that I felt I could be doing more. It was frustrating for me to work out of someone else's space and pay them 50% of my earnings. I had very little autonomy in decision making for how I ran my routine. I was told when to work, how many clients I had to take in a day, and sometimes I was even asked to cover for another therapist if they called in sick. Even though I very much enjoyed what I did and the ability to earn money based on commission, I didn't enjoy giving half of that income away while not having much say in how I ran my own career. Now don't get me wrong, I was and am very grateful for this time in my life because I learned a lot about the industry working there, including how to run a business, *and* how *not* to run a business.

After six months, the owners of the clinic had let me know that I was getting a 10% increase in my commission, so now I was on a 60/40% split; 60 to me, 40 to the owners. While this was good news, it still didn't correct the fact that I was giving away a large chunk of money for a small space and very little business decision making power. In fact, I very much felt like an employee within my own career and that just wasn't sitting right with me. I didn't want someone controlling my hours, how much I could charge, how I dressed, and the routine they thought I should have with my scheduled day.

All the initial newness of being in my career and being able to develop my skills and learn about how I like to run things was amazing, but the restricted nature of working for someone else started to take its toll on me. During my client sessions, I found that I was daydreaming more about what my own business would look like and how I would operate it. I started to realize that I was an entrepreneur and that part of me was unsatisfied with my current situation. I wanted to earn more, do more and create more with my career and have the freedom to make the decisions on where I was headed.

SHIFT IN AWARENESS

So, I spent months feeling unhappy, unsatisfied and under the control of someone else's business. I was building someone else's dream and I wanted to have my own! However, I wasn't really doing anything about it other than just wanting. This wanting and feeling of being unhappy started to show up in other ways for me. I felt irritable, and I began feeling more defiant about the decisions the clinic owners were making. I was voicing my opinion more and more.

I found myself one night while at home on my computer, browsing the internet when I came across an article that talked about depression and understanding yourself through hypnotherapy. There was a clinical hypnotherapist in my area and because I resonated with the information in the article, I decided to book a session.

This is when my life completely changed, as this experience shaped me into who I am today and sparked a new passion that I didn't even know I had.

A powerful awareness and learning happened in that session that gave me a brand-new concept around how my mind processed information and why I was feeling the way I was. I learned that my focus on my unhappiness was keeping me in the same spot and restricting me from freedom. I learned that the beliefs that were instilled in me from when I was a child and throughout my adolescence from my environment, were already creating my results on a deeper level.

Don't get me wrong, I have amazingly supportive and loving parents, but like anyone, they also have their own beliefs about success and accomplishment that were adopted by the influential people in their lives.

THE PUSH TO DECIDE

A few weeks after that hypnotherapy session, I was asked to stay behind for 20 minutes after wrapping up my last client for the day. I had a feeling something was up because of the strange tension I had been sensing leading up to that moment.

"Richard, this isn't working out and we don't think you're a good fit for working here."

I was devastated! I felt betrayed, hurt, rejected and like I wasn't good enough. I knew I was an excellent massage therapist, so it didn't have to do with my skills. It had everything to do with the fact that my true nature of being an entrepreneur was trying to get out. Near the end of the meeting, their parting words to me were, "If you're thinking about going into business for yourself, we are your largest competition and will put you out of business, so you should save yourself the time and energy and go find another clinic to work out of instead."

Something inside of me woke up in that moment. I went from feeling like a victim to feeling like I now had a mission to prove everyone wrong. I didn't like being told what to do before this, and that was a big part of why they were letting me go. So, that wasn't going to change now. I wasn't going to let them tell me what I should or shouldn't do even after I left! I decided in that very moment that all the imagining and mental planning I had been doing for the past year was going to be turned into a solid goal and action plan!

I was scared, oh man was I ever! I felt like I had zero clue on how to run my own business and even know where to start. What if I fail? What if they are in fact my biggest competition and they put me out of business within the first year? What if I cannot afford to do this? What if I look like a complete fool?

While all these were legitimate fears I was having, I had felt these emotions before and overcame them. In fact, I have felt those same emotions around anything new and big that I was about to undergo. It reminded me of my very first client, the pregnant one that I thought I was going to kill through my massage! The feeling was EXACTLY THE SAME; it just had a different dialogue attached to it. But, overall, fear is fear regardless of the story around it.

Also, at this point, I had to make a major decision between two options right away:

Take the leap and start my own business, even though I didn't have a plan or know how I was going to do it OR...

Start handing out resumes and hope that another clinic would pick me up.

See, the problem with the second option is that it would just be me going right back into the same scenario that I was unhappy with in the first place. Really, I would be letting my fear tell me to stick with what I knew, stay in the safety net of someone else's business. I could still live off working for someone else and feel happy, right? Wrong. That's not living, that's settling and just barely surviving.

After leaving that meeting and going through all the emotions, I decided that I was going to do it; I was going to open my own business regardless of not knowing how it was going to turn out or even how I was going to do it. I come from a family of entrepreneurs, people who started from nothing and created empires because they believed in their dreams, and more importantly, they believed in themselves. I called up my mother who, at the time, was a reflexologist working from home part time.

"Mum, I just called to let you know that I decided to start my own massage therapy practice and I would love for you to be part of it."

AND THEN A BUSINESS WAS BORN

In that moment, my business was born. I spent the next few weeks doing a lot of writing and planning of what I wanted this business to look and feel like. I planned out the type of physical space I wanted, what I wanted the feeling of it to be, the type of people I wanted to work with me, and the type of clients I wanted to have coming to my clinic. Everything seemed to fall into place like magic. Of course, there were obstacles, adversities, and setbacks, but it was all part of the larger journey into entrepreneurship and learning how to start a new business.

So, you're probably wondering what ever happened to the clinic I first started at, and if my former employers ever did put me out of business. The short answer is that they were open for a few more years, then they closed their doors.

My business on the other hand, did very well and lasted many years before I shifted my path into another career. I had my own beautiful space, made my own hours, made more money than I ever had before, sold my own product and overall, made all my own decisions. Within the first year of opening my practice, I had other massage therapists working out of it and of course, a reflexologist (my mother). I made a point as well that I would start them off on a 60/40 percentage split (60% to them and 40% to me) with a reasonable cap. None of this "whatever you earn I'm taking half of," nonsense. It's all about knowing your value and your worth, while keeping those who help you build your business happy and helping them grow towards their own success.

I was waking up in the mornings excited to go back to what I created for myself and to keep building on it. Others came to rent a space from me, which gave me more freedom to go away on vacation if I wanted to, while I was putting additional passive income back into MY business.

If I had given into that fear of failure or that fear of competition, then I wouldn't have gone through that amazing experience and learned what I needed to learn about myself and creating a new business.

That life experience was just the start of what was in the cards for me, and it was by far the scariest, but best thing I ever decided to do.

"Wealthy entrepreneurs understand that success is not a secret, it's a system, and the biggest part of that system is understanding how to use your mind to create the results you want."

CHAPTER 3

"Success is not a secret, it's a system."

Overview of the principles I use to be successful with my own goals, big and small.

I believe that people either do things consciously or unconsciously. So, they can decide to create the dynamic of the career they really want by being clear on their wants, mapping out their objectives and moving towards that image. Or, they can unconsciously move towards their wants through their own built-in autopilot. The problem with the latter is that there are no conscious decisions involved. It's kind of like sailing your boat without an engine, and just allowing the winds and the currents to lead you to where you're hopefully meant to be. This isn't always a bad thing, but if you have any limiting thoughts and beliefs about yourself, those winds might push you into places that you don't really want to be.

A couple of years ago, one of my mentors named Bob Proctor said, "Success is not a secret, it's a system." This really resonated with me in the sense that if you ever want to understand success, study others who are successful. What do they do each day? What are their routines? What are their beliefs about themselves that push them to where they want to be?

I worked with Bob Proctor for awhile as one of his consultants, and the insights I have gained from this man have been nothing short of awe inspiring. I learned about the principles of success and how to apply them within my own life. I understood that when I was a practicing massage therapy entrepreneur, I was being what's known as an "unconscious competent," meaning that I was on auto pilot with where I was going, but because I already had a structured success mindset and a drive to accomplish my goal, I was able to reach my destination with relative ease.

The only problem with being an "unconscious competent" is that the skill is non-transferable. That means that I didn't really know exactly how I did it, I just knew that I did it. Therefore, at the time, if I wanted to coach someone on how to do the same, I probably wouldn't have been effective at relaying the information. Before I learned what I know now, I didn't understand some of the principles that you are going to learn in this book. I know, without a fraction of a doubt, that if I had understood these principles on achieving goals, I would have reached much higher than I actually did, and I probably wouldn't have taken so long to make the decision either.

THE SUCCESS PRINCIPLES I USE
WITH MY OWN GOALS

The system that you are going to learn throughout this book is broken up into sections. These principles are what I use today with all my goals, big and small, and they are the basis of all that I teach to my students. Having systems and a structure in how you set and achieve goals is so important. They create intent on where you want to go, and they steer you into the right direction, so that it is inevitable that you arrive.

If you have vague goals without clarity and without a process for reaching those goals, then you are not harnessing the miraculous abilities we all have in accomplishing what you previously believed was not possible for yourself. If a goal is left without a structure, the same end result that could take a very short period of time to reach could take years or might never be reached at all.

Having clarity about what you want in your massage career is a vitally important first step in your entrepreneurial endeavour. I am going to take you in-depth into understanding what it is your truly want and how to articulate it in a way that, even if you were to explain it to a complete stranger, they would have a clear mental image of what your goal actually is.

When you have any goal in mind, you are always going to be up against limiting beliefs in how you are going to achieve that goal. Through this process, you are going to learn how to identify where those limiting beliefs come from, and how to replace them with more supporting, goal achieving thoughts that you can harness which will push you effortlessly to where you really want to be.

One of the aspects around this process you're about to learn has had the most profound effect on my own success and that of my clients. It's the identification of habits that either bring you closer to where you want to be or push you further away. Often, we aren't even aware of our own non-productive habits, but I want you to understand that 95% of what we do and the results we get in our lives, is habitual. This means your habits are going to be the determining factor to your successes, or your struggles.

What about fear and how does fear play into all of this? Where does it come from and why does it debilitate you from making big moves towards what you really want for yourself? I know firsthand like you do, just how awful fear can feel when it prevents you from living the life you want to live. Fear itself is a by-product of a mental programming that can be re-programmed, and I'm going to raise your awareness of exactly how you can do this and move through it. I'll show you how to move from fear, to freedom.

I often hear from many different success gurus that if you want to be successful, you must act like you're successful. Easier said than done, right? Well, it all comes down to your own self-image of how you feel about yourself. It's about your perceptions.

Are you really acting like the person that is the successful massage therapy business owner that you want to be? The therapist who has other practitioners wanting and begging to work for your thriving business? We are going to explore a bit later in this book how your self-image impacts your success, and how you can create a new improved self-image, so you can embody and amplify those wonderful aspects of yourself in your everyday life.

Have you ever considered that you might not want certain types of clients in your practice? Being clear around the type of client you want to attract to your business is also going to be a very important aspect to become aware of and to understand. Once you become clear on your ideal clients, it becomes easier for you to attract them to your business. Do you see a theme here? Everything is about clarity and specificity. I'm going to show you how to gain that clarity about the type of clients you enjoy the most, and that clarity is going to help your business thrive, not just survive.

There is a universal importance of service to others. If there wasn't, you wouldn't be the massage therapist you are right now or working towards that. You are a healer because you enjoy helping people heal. I'm sure they are out there, but I have yet to meet a massage therapist who does what they do because they just feel like giving massages. You provide a service to others who can benefit from what you have to give. I will highlight exactly how you can harness this natural ability that you already possess to create more abundance within your business and even in your personal life.

There is something to be said about power in numbers. Earlier, I mentioned that if you ever want to understand success, study others who are successful. I'm going to teach you how you can harness the ideas and skills of others so that they complement your own goals and where you are headed and create wonderful connections and friendships by doing so. We are going to dive into the "Mastermind Principle", made popular by Napoleon Hill's book, *Think and Grow Rich*. I, along with many others, use this principle to overcome problems and adversities within our businesses. In fact, one of America's most successful entrepreneurs, Andrew Carnegie, attributes almost all his successes to the Mastermind Principle.

Always remember that it's not luck that will get you to your career goal, or any goal for that matter; it's a system. If you follow the system, do the work and remain dedicated to it, I guarantee that you will accomplish much more than just the goal you set out to achieve. You will open doors for yourself that you didn't even know were there, all because you decided to work on yourself and move towards the success you are inherently born to have.

"THE PURPOSE OF A GOAL IS TO GROW INTO SOMEONE WHO YOU ARE CURRENTLY NOT IN YOUR PRESENT STATE, PERIOD."

CHAPTER 4

Your Big Goal

*Learn about what a goal really is and how
to set, then achieve the right goal for you.*

First, I want you to think carefully about something here. What I'm about to ask you can determine how what you want unfolds in the way you expect it to, and it can create the difference between the start of a planned-out endeavour, or just an idea that stays in your mind.

Have you become very clear with your business goal, and if so, do you have it written down?

I ask this because even though this concept of formulating a goal might seem so simple, many people are not aware of how powerful and directional this topic is for their success. Put this to the test for yourself and go ask 10 people today what their goal is for their career. I can almost guarantee that over half do not actually have a clearly defined goal. Most of them probably have just a general idea of what they want, and even if they have a clear vision of this thing they want, chances are they do not have that goal written down on paper.

BECOME VERY CLEAR WITH YOUR GOALS

Writing causes some amazing things to happen inside the brain, and for your mind in general. Articulating your goal onto paper causes you to slow down and become mentally clear with what it is you're wanting. Writing is also a form of creativity and the start to any sort of physical manifestation towards your desired end result.

If someone were to ask you what your career goal was, what would you say? Would you be able to tell them with absolute clarity, so that the person you're sharing it with can create a clear image in their own mind through your description?

If you're unable to clearly define this goal of yours, then I highly recommend that we start right away and determine what this dream business of yours looks like. But first, let's talk a little bit about what a goal is and why setting the right type of goal is so important for the success of what you're wanting.

When I first started working with Bob Proctor, he taught me about three different types of goals and why some entrepreneurs do not create the success that they're capable of reaching. These are the goals which are most commonly set by individuals, and I want to structure how I understand this information in a way that it's easy for you to understand.

THE THREE TYPES OF GOALS

Let's break these types of goals down a little bit so you can see if you are setting your goals too low, or if you are reaching for that massive success that I know you're capable of achieving.

Familiar Goals

A familiar goal is something you have already done before. For example, maybe you're thinking about going back for some continuing education to get a certification in another modality which complements your massage therapy designation. You decide that you're going to move ahead, invest your time and money, then take the course. The familiar goal doesn't have any growth in it. It's something you already know how to do, and it doesn't really provide any type of challenge because you already have the skills and the know-how to accomplish it.

Predictable Goals

A predictable goal is something that you have not done before, but you determine its achievability based on the conditions of your environment. Picture the massage business you want to start, which I assume you can since you're reading this book.

You set your goal based on many external and environmental factors such as how the economy is doing, how much money you might have in your bank account, your education, your time spent as a massage therapist, and other's opinions on what you should and shouldn't do based on their own experience and fears.

These goals might grow you a bit, but they're going to be limited based on what your external environment tells you, not what you are really wanting for yourself. A predictable goal doesn't challenge you to shift your perspective or your self-image to obtain the result of that goal.

Did you know that some of the most successful businesses started in times of economic downturn and hardship?

These entrepreneurs shifted their perception from that of fear and limitation, to looking for opportunity to build on something amazing. Don't believe me? Feel free to go online and research businesses that started within an economic crisis or downturn; you will find hundreds to inspire you.

Predictable goals are laden with conditions based on what currently is, not what could be possible for you.

Audacious Goals

Audacious goals are your BIG goals, and these are the goals that I encourage you to work towards with my help through reading this book.

These are the "what do you REALLY want" type of goals. No wildly successful entrepreneur sets his or her sights low and limited. They persisted on their vision and created it to happen for themselves, despite what they had done before or what their external environment and the people in it were telling them.

Your big audacious goal should be something that you have no idea how you're going to do it, but all you know if that it's something that ignites a burning desire within you, and the thought alone of accomplishing it makes you feel amazing.

If it doesn't scare and excite you at the same time, then it's probably not worth doing and it's definitely not an audacious goal.

The primary purpose of a goal is to grow into someone who you are currently not in your present state, period. Do not worry about the dreaded "how" details of that goal; that will come into your awareness once you make the decision that you're going to work towards that vision. It always does!

The person you are right now is not the same person who has achieved that goal in the future, so trying to determine all the finer details of how you're going to reach your audacious goal as the person you are now will only set you up for giving up. It's crucial that you understand this, because your old mental programming will keep you stuck where you are as it is resistant to change.

I want you to think of a time in your life when you were scared to do something, but you knew that once you got over that fear and just did it, your life would be improved in some way on the other side of just doing it. Maybe it was booking your very first client, or even bigger, like leaving your salary job and going back to school to better your education and open up more opportunities.

Do you think that if you allowed your fearful thoughts to take over and make those decisions for you, that you would be who you are today? No. You would be the same person you were years before, making the same choices, completing the same actions, and having the same outcomes. Zero growth there and keeps you stuck in a repetitive loop of repeating unwanted results.

ENVISION YOUR GOAL

Before you go onto the next chapter, I want you to take some time where you will not be disturbed, get into a comfortable position, and think about your goal. Imagine that you had no obstacles in your way to achieving this goal, then think about how you want your massage therapy practice to look like, and why.

Who is in this vision of yours, and why? What does your business model look like, and why? Are you in a clinic/center or are you mobile, and why? Do you have multiple locations with multiple employees, or are you a one-person show, and why?

The "why" aspect here is important, because when you have a strong reason for what you want, it helps you become even clearer, and it also helps attach a positive emotion to the image you are creating. You will understand later why that positive emotion plays such a pivotal role in the creation of your goal.

Next, write out all your business wants and desires on a piece of paper. Narrow those wants down to things you have never done before, and you have no idea how to do them. Narrow, it down even further to the few that bring up an excited "I would just love that" type of feeling inside of you. Really feel what that vision looks like in your mind and the sensations in your body and don't over analyze it.

Allow yourself to play a little bit here, like a child would with their imagination. Tap into that emotion of success and having something bigger and better than what you have right now.

Once you have a clearer image in your mind of your audacious goal, I want you to write out in a short paragraph the summary of that image. So, it might be something like this

"I have a successful massage therapy practice which services many happy paying clients each week and allows me to have the freedom to spend more time doing the things I love to do. I am now earning an abundance of passive income, while I work less and make more money."

This is the type of general, but clear statement that I have my students create when they work directly with me through my *Massage Therapist Success Fundamentals* program, which this book is based on. It acts as an affirmation statement to your bigger goal. We will talk more about how all of this fits into your own mental programming and conditioning later in the book. But for now, let's get your momentum started by creating that safe space for the mental image of what you truly want for yourself in your massage career.

It's important to note that when writing out your wants, desires, and ultimately your goal statement, to only speak positive aspects. Avoid the limiting "I don't want" statements, as your subconscious mind is only aware of what you focus on and will amplify aspects within your environment that bring you closer to that focus. So, for this reason, being specific is very important. I will delve into more on the subconscious mind in the next chapter.

Now that you understand your wants and have a clearer, more defined goal, set aside ten minutes first thing each morning when you wake up, and write out that goal statement.

Doing this while your mind is still coming out of what's known as a theta state, will help you set your intention and absorb it deeper into your subconscious mind, so it can begin to carry out that desired command you have placed inside it.

Then, carry that goal statement with you on a goal card and read it throughout the day as often as possible. This continues to reinforce that set intention and begins to bury it deep in your mind. After a short period of time, you should be able to speak your goal statement verbatim without having to read it off the card.

You cannot reach your goal without action, so I have included at the end of this book a link to get your free goal setting lesson video as my gift to you.

"BEFORE YOU BEGIN ANY
SORT OF ACTION TOWARD
YOUR AUDACIOUS GOAL, YOU
FIRST NEED TO IDENTIFY THE
LIMITING BELIEF THAT HOLDS
THE OPPOSITE OPINION OF WHAT
YOU'RE WANTING TO ACHIEVE."

CHAPTER 5

The Power of Paradigms

What is a paradigm and how does it control almost all the results we get in life?

W hat if you were able to sit down and map out all the things you want to accomplish in your career, then watch those things begin to form themselves into your life experience right in front of your eyes. Would you want to learn how to do that? Well, in this book I'm going to show you exactly how.

But first, in order for you to be able to have the skill to consciously choose and create the events and circumstances you want to happen in your life, you need to understand how your mind creates anything in the first place.

Make no mistake, you are already doing this but you're just not aware you're doing it.

You are a brilliant master of creating thoughts into things, but the problem is that you may be on auto pilot like 96% of the people on this planet. Isn't it interesting how approximately 1% of the population earns 96% of all the money earned? Why is that?

It's because these wealthy entrepreneurs understand that success is not a secret, it's a system, and the biggest part of that system is understanding how to use the power of your mind to create the results you want.

THE STICK PERSON

Let's dive deeper into some aspects of the mind for a minute, so we can have a better grasp on what you're dealing with exactly. I want to introduce to you a concept that was created by Dr. Thurman Fleet, who was a brilliant chiropractor and healer in the 1930's in San Antonio, Texas.

Dr. Fleet's process around how to heal the body was so popular, he had to move his practice three times to remain in concert with the occupancy fire codes at the time. His offices were filled with people coming to see him from far and wide, because word got out that Dr. Fleet was able to heal his patients of almost any disease that inflicted them.

Dr. Fleet understood that if you wanted to change your outcome, you needed to change your mind. But the problem was that for anyone to change something, they had to first understand what it is they are changing.

After contemplating that problem and realising that we think in pictures, Dr Fleet created the concept of the Stick Person. Now he had a diagram of what the mind looked like that he could show his patients.

With this image, he was able to explain to his patients how we think, and how our thoughts are forming our future outcomes. It was then that his patients began to see dramatic improvements not only in their physical ailments, but in most other areas of their lives as well.

The stick person illustrates the reality that you have a power inside of you that is much greater than any circumstance or condition in your life. It shows you that you can literally direct this power through your own thoughts, to create whatever outcome you desire. The trick here is understanding and applying it to yourself.

Although the image below, which is a representation of Dr. Fleet's diagram, might seem quite simple and elementary, I caution you against dismissing the impact which I know it is going on have on your journey. Bob Proctor showcases this diagram in even more detail in his book *It's Not About the Money*, which is where I was first introduced to this visual concept.

This diagram is going to help you understand the process that a thought goes through, in how it literally creates the reality you live in. If you allow it to, it can open an awareness inside of you and open many doors to wonderful and prosperous possibilities in your life.

THE CONSCIOUS MIND
(The Analytical Thinking Mind)

The top half of the diagram is what is known as your conscious mind. This is the part of your mind that you do most of your daily thinking from, the part where you reason with the information that is coming in from your external environment. This is also the part of your mind where your free will resides, where you can choose and decide what you want to do, and where you want to apply your focus.

Your sensory factors allow you to interact with your external environment through sight, sound, hearing, smelling, tasting, and touching. Remember that 96% of the population we were talking about earlier? Well, those people allow these stimuli from the outside world to determine and direct their thoughts, which has them focusing on "what is" vs. "what could be."

The great thing about being human is that we have something called free will, which allows us to direct our thoughts anywhere we like. So, we are not slaves to the order of what our environment tells us about ourselves and we can direct those thoughts to any area we wish. Many wise practitioners throughout centuries understood this and use tools like meditation and mindfulness to learn how to consciously choose and control what they want their thoughts to focus on.

The conscious mind is all about accepting or rejecting ideas and understanding that no person or circumstance can force you into thinking any thoughts that you truly do not want. This can be one of the most liberating and powerful pieces of information that I will ever share with you. The reason why this is so powerful, and liberating, is because it doesn't matter if those thoughts are directed from inside of you, or outside of you, they will eventually through repetition determine the results you get in your career.

When you accept any thought in your conscious mind, it then becomes impressed upon the subconscious mind and controls 95% of the outcomes you get.

SUBCONSCIOUS MIND (The Programmable Mind)

The bottom half of the diagram represents the subconscious mind. I would like to make an important note that the subconscious mind is present in every cell of your body, but for this diagram, we will show it as the lower half of the stick person's head.

I could probably create an entire program and write a whole book about the subconscious mind alone, but for this book, we will cover the most important aspects of this subject that will apply directly to you, and what you're wanting to achieve from it within your own massage therapy career.

I want you to think about your subconscious mind like a hard drive in a computer, and your conscious mind like the user of that computer (you). The conscious mind creates the program (thought) and the subconscious mind implements that program through something we call a paradigm, which I will get into momentarily.

One of the most fascinating things that you will discover about the subconscious mind is that it has no ability to reject the information it is given, only accept. This means that anytime you begin to repetitively impress a conscious thought on the subconscious mind, it reinforces an existing running program, OR it begins to create a new one entirely.

Your subconscious mind also cannot tell the difference between if something is actually happening to you, or if it's something you're imagining. A good example of this would be to imagine right now that you have a fresh lemon sitting in front of you. You take a knife and cut the lemon into four quarters, and you bring a slice of that lemon up to your mouth. Imagine smelling that lemon, then touch it to your lips, and take a bite out of the slice allowing the sour, tart juice from the lemon to enter your mouth.

Did your jaw start to tingle, even a little bit? Did your mouth begin to salivate? Did you have an emotional reaction to this? This is an example of the subconscious mind thinking that what you're imagining is actually happening, so it creates a physical response.

Now, if that works with just a thought of biting into a sour lemon, then imagine how it responds to negative memories, or feared future outcomes that haven't physically happened yet. You know consciously that what you think is imagined, but your subconscious mind thinks its real. Your subconscious activates neurons in your brain which signals the release of hormones that activate a stress response in the body. Replaying negative past situations creates your body to believe you're living that moment in the present, even if you're not.

The programs running within your subconscious mind (paradigms), have almost exclusive control over all of the results you get in your career, relationships, health, self-image, everything.

WHY IS THIS?

Because the subconscious mind operates on these paradigms as facts, it will physically guide you based on this information (without you even being consciously aware of it) to the people, events and situations that validate the program it has running. Your subconscious essentially looks in your external environment for circumstances and situations to match the belief, and then creates a result to be more of the same.

An example of a subconscious program might be, "Every time I try to get ahead with my business, something happens that sets me back." Or, "It is so hard getting new clients in this city because of all the competition out there." These are running programs that are reflected into your reality because your subconscious mind guides you through your own actions, to things in your environment that validate that current belief.

THE BODY
(The Physical Expression of the Mind)

Your body is the physical expression of your mind. It's the vessel your mind uses in the physical to move towards its programmed desired result. Your conscious mind thinks a thought that is impressed on the subconscious mind. The subconscious mind then creates a vibration in the body based on that thought program that is running; we call this an emotion or feeling. This is done within a fraction of a second without you even noticing it's happening.

That emotion creates a behavior, which is expressed through your actions and ultimately determines your life outcomes and results.

Let's summarize and simplify this a little more: **Thoughts > Feelings > Actions = Results**

So, now that you have a basic awareness of how you get the results you do in your career and life in general, you can now begin to move down the path to changing your current results to the ones you want. You will begin to practice choosing different thoughts to create new neural pathways in the brain, which creates new feelings and emotions, which produces different results and outcomes for you.

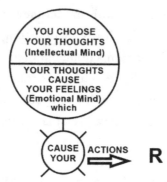

PARADIGM (subconscious programming)

From this point forward, anytime I mention paradigm to you, I am talking about the directive you have running in your subconscious mind, which is responsible for almost all the results (**R**) you get in your life.

So, what is a paradigm? A paradigm is a multitude of habits imbedded in your subconscious mind. 95% of what you do is habitual, from the side of the bed you get out of in the morning, to the way you walk, to how you brush your hair, and even which shoe you put on first.

Paradigms control almost all your outcomes because they control your actions, reactions and responses to outside stimuli in your environment.

So, how did we get these paradigms in the first place? Well, up until around the age of 7 or 8 we are pretty much an open well for downloading information from our environment. That is why we end up being very similar to our parents, or authority figures we grew up with in our lives.

Look at some of the most influential people in your life when you were a child and ask yourself, "What beliefs did that person have about themselves and their life, that I also have about myself and my life?"

It's through the repetition of this observed, learned behaviour, where these paradigms are created. They impact us into our adult lives, sometimes even through to the end of our lives. The good news here is that a paradigm can be changed if your desire to change it is strong enough.

Many years ago, on the side of being a massage therapist, I was also a practicing Clinical Hypnotherapist, and I primarily helped people with releasing fears, phobias, and some addictive behaviors. The way I did this was through guiding them into a very relaxed state of mind, which for the most part would bypass the conscious analytical mind, so I could get right to the subconscious paradigm and reprogram it from there.

This proved time and time again to be very effective, but in order for someone to really change their results, they had to come in sometimes for multiple sessions, and it wasn't really something they were empowered to do on their own.

Through my process now, I show my students who are wanting to make big changes in their results how to do so consciously. The trick to all of this, is to use how it started in the first place; repetition of thought.

To change your paradigm, you must go back to the system of how it was created, which is through exposed repetition of thought. If a paradigm is a subconscious belief, and a belief is just something you tell yourself over and over, then you can use that exact same principle to create new beliefs and new paradigms.

"BEGIN TO CREATE NEW ACTIONS WHICH EVENTUALLY FORM NEW HABITS THAT CHALLENGES AND WEAKENS THE OLD LIMITING PARADIGM, UNTIL IT IS NO LONGER THE DOMINANT BEHAVIOR PRESENT."

CHAPTER 6

Habits

How to determine what your non-productive habits are, and how to replace them with productive, goal-achieving routines.

I n the last chapter, I talked to you about the mind and the operating program called a paradigm. I mentioned to you that a paradigm is a multitude of habits, and that 95% of what we do in our waking hours is habitual and therefore controlled by this subconscious mental programming.

There is a massive difference between what we know, and what we do. In fact, this is so accurate that I bet you know a handful of people with degrees and certifications coming off the end of their email signature, yet they're not doing too well in their careers. Or maybe you know someone who has a full knowledge and understanding of how to lose weight, but for some reason, jumps between small losses then back to becoming their overweight self. This all has to do with these "multitude of habits" I've been talking about.

I want you to think for a moment that you do indeed choose that you are going to step out of your normal comfortable routine and start working towards new and better results. In this case, it would be the obvious goal of becoming your own boss and business owner. Now, you understand that you are running on a specific paradigm that is creating a behavior inside of you, which in turn is controlling your actions through habitual patterns and thus creating the results you're currently getting.

The part of you that is a thriving business owner does not operate on the same subconscious programming that you are currently operating through; if it was, then you wouldn't be reading this book and we wouldn't be having this conversation right now, as you would already be where you want to be. You need to be able to consciously start impressing the new directives you want your subconscious to being adopting, in order to change the old paradigm that is currently running. Whether you know it or not, you have already started this process through the clarification of your big audacious goal you began working on earlier.

Your self-image of how you look already having this reality is an important aspect of this; however, we will talk more about that later in chapter 8.

YOUR EXISTING HABITS

First, I am going to address with you the interruption of the existing paradigm's habits that are no longer serving you in your life. At one point it would have served you, but like your phone or your computer, software upgrades are necessary if you want a faster, more efficient running machine that provides better results than what you were previously getting.

The start of any change comes from the awareness of what it is you are changing. This is so that you do not let the old familiar non-productive habits unwittingly creep in and sabotage the creation of the new paradigm that you're wanting to embody. It's important that you take a moment to identify that old running paradigm and the habits that are attached to it.

For example, maybe you have a paradigm that tells you it is difficult to attract repeat clients to your practice. Therefore, understanding this belief you currently have, you look at the actions you do, or avoid doing, that reinforce that reality you are creating through that old mental programming.

Maybe one of those non-productive habits might be instead of following up with the client a few days after their treatment, you spend that time browsing the internet looking for the perfect Christmas gift for your partner, even though Christmas is three months away!

That is a non-productive action or habit that isn't in alignment with what you want as part of your larger business goal. Yes, procrastination is indeed a habit and so is avoidance. Why would you bother following up with a client if you already have an active belief that it's hard to get repeat clients into your business? In your internal reality, there is no point in making that effort, so you do something else.

Can you see the connection now between how the paradigm creates habits that are in alignment with its current programming? This is true with every single paradigm you have in your mind, and you have hundreds of them, if not thousands.

So, before you begin any sort of actions towards your business and career goals, you first need to identify the paradigm that holds the opposite belief of what you're wanting to achieve.

Let's go over a few more examples of some goals that might have opposing existing paradigms.

Goal – "I am a successful massage therapy entrepreneur who earns 5x my previous yearly income."

Existing Paradigm – "I have to work extremely long hours to earn more money and I won't have time to do the things I enjoy. It's just too hard and I will fail."

Goal – "I own a mobile massage business and I employ several mobile massage therapists who in turn earn me fantastic passive income, allowing me to do the things I really want to do within my business and personal life."

Existing Paradigm – "There is so much competition out there that I won't make it in that type of business. I might as well stay working for someone else where I can avoid the failure, shame and disappointment."

Goal – "I now work out of my home doing massage therapy and because of that, I have very little overhead, I can make my own hours and can write off some of my home expenses under my business."

Existing Paradigm – "Clients won't want to come to my house, that's just weird. There are too many distractions here and I'm not sure I want people to know where I live."

Your existing paradigm will do whatever it takes to talk you out of working towards your new goal.

Remember when I said if a goal doesn't scare and excite you at the same time, it's probably not worth doing? Well, that scary part is almost always your old paradigm trying to stay active and alive. It will present some very convincing arguments based on your fears to keep you where you are, in the familiar and the routine you already have.

UNDERSTANDING YOUR OLD PARADIGMS

Once you have identified your old paradigms and the messages they give to you to keep you stuck where you are, you can then truly understand them for what they really represent, old limiting programs imbedded in your subconscious mind.

Maxwell Maltz in his book **Psycho Cybernetics** put it best when he said:

> *A human being always acts and feels and performs in accordance with what he imagines to be true about himself and his environment...For imagination sets the goal 'picture' which our automatic mechanism works on. We act, or fail to act, not because of 'will,' as is so commonly believed, but because of imagination.*

The old paradigm, or automatic mechanism in this case, of what you can and cannot do was created first and foremost through our external environment as children, and then was often reinforced through our repetitive thought processes as adults. The old limiting paradigm will place "what ifs" and self doubt images into your conscious awareness. This has enormous power and control over our future thinking, which is unknowingly almost always in harmony with that old paradigm.

Understanding your old paradigm and the limitations it places on you, places you back into the driver's seat. You now become the programmer to the program and turn off the auto pilot switch on what no longer propels you forward into the career you want to have, and the life you want to live.

So, how do you change the old paradigm that isn't in alignment with your goal?

...Well, there are three ways to do this.

First is through an intense emotional impact which creates a shock to the mind. Unfortunately, these occurrences are almost always negative. We can use post traumatic stress disorder as an example of this.

Second is through the therapeutic help of someone like a clinical hypnotherapist, where the therapist can bypass the conscious analytical mind and implant suggestions for the subconscious mind to take hold of. Think of that like a direct download of a new program. This sometimes takes multiple sessions to accomplish, depending on the strength of the old program.

And **third**, what we are working on here and as mentioned in the last chapter, is the conscious repetition of what it is you really want to embody. When you do this, you will begin to successfully alter the existing paradigm. The trick here though is to stick with it, because like how physical fitness shapes your body, it doesn't happen within just a week of exercise. You must constantly bombard your subconscious mind with the repetition of the statement, and emotion, of where you're wanting to go and who you're striving to become.

Then, you must identify the non-productive habits you know are not in alignment with this new paradigm you're working to embed into your subconscious mind. You're going to interrupt and replace those non-productive habits with their counter opposite, as it's the opposite of the non-productive habits that you want to focus on and practice.

So, if your old limiting paradigm tells you that it's too hard to get repeat clients into your business, then you must be working on consciously replacing it with the new paradigm which tells you how easy and effortless it is to get repeat clients through your doors. Then, you can be consciously aware that instead of buying Christmas gifts online, you set aside 10 to 15 minutes once per week to follow up with all the clients who didn't re-book the week before. The new action which works outside of what you typically would do, yields new results.

You begin to create new actions which eventually form a new habit, which challenges and weakens the old paradigm until it is no longer the dominant behavior producing unwanted results.

New thought > New emotion/behavior > New actions = New results

WORD OF CAUTION

It is important that you only work on one or two habits at a time. In most cases with my students, I find that if they work on changing multiple habits at once, the mind becomes overwhelmed and the paradigm begins to really bring out the big guns to stay alive. You then begin to find reasons to procrastinate and then beat yourself up, and that creates a bundle of negative emotions which keeps you stuck even more.

To combat this, do the following simple exercise, and from it you will see some amazing progress towards the results you want.

Sit down and really think about your audacious goal. Describe that goal, and the ideal end date for reaching that goal.

Write out your "why's" and tap into the emotion of what it would mean to you to have accomplished this goal, and what it will do for your life.

Close your eyes and imagine yourself having already achieved that goal. Who are you in this image? Who is around you? What type of life are you living? What does your daily routine look like? How do you feel?

Write down the actions or steps that you need to start taking that will bring you closer to this end goal. When you have completed writing them down, prioritize that list.

TAKE ACTION! The night before, take one or two of those productive action items and make a commitment to yourself that the following day, you are going to accomplish or begin to work on accomplishing one of those steps. If the task is a larger task, break that down into smaller productive actions until you accomplish that task. This gets the momentum shifted towards your end goal and gets that ball rolling.

YOU'RE BECOMING A BETTER VERSION OF YOU

It's so important that you are kind and patient with yourself. Be your own biggest cheerleader. The simple fact that you're making productive action steps towards a clearly defined goal, is a massive progression from where you were before you started.

I was having a conversation the other day with a student of mine who had told me that she started towards a goal, then had to take a step back a few months later and analyze just how far she has come with her goals. She said to me that she didn't realize how much she had accomplished because it was her new normal.

This reminded me that when you are in the place where you want to be or working towards that big goal of yours, you are indeed becoming a different person, a better version of yourself. All the actions you are taking which are in harmony with your new paradigm, are feeling very much like second nature to you. It's because you are no longer that person who set those goals with that old paradigm controlling you, that seemed so scary and unachievable before. You are the person who is well on the path to achieving that end goal.

And when that end goal comes, you start the process all over again. Part of the beauty around all of this, and being human, is that you are always growing, in ALL-WAYS.

Now, I want you to go back and identify those limiting old paradigms that are not serving your new audacious goal and become aware of exactly how they might try and sabotage that goal of yours. Then consciously become aware of the actions that your new paradigm would embody and write them down.

Work on one or two of those new actions each day and form them into new productive habits, then watch those wanted results begin to manifest!

"FEAR IS A DREAM KILLER
FOR MOST, BUT WHEN YOU
UNDERSTAND WHAT FEAR
MEANS, WHERE IT COMES FROM
AND WHY, THEN YOU CAN
UTILIZE IT TO KNOW YOU'RE
ON THE RIGHT TRACK."

CHAPTER 7

The Dream Killer, or the Internal Compass?

Understanding your own fears around starting a business and how to use that destructive emotion to your advantage.

I want to talk to you about something that is not only a dream killer, but it's also responsible for almost everything negative in this world: fear. Now, don't get me wrong here, fear can be very healthy depending on the type of fear.

The way I look at it is that you are living with two fear types:

Survival fear where your intuition tells you that you need to either do something or not do something for physical safety reasons, and...

Perceived outcome fear regarding growth and development of one's self.

The two are very different and both do serve a purpose, just one more-so than the other.

I do not recommend moving through fear if you know there is a chance you can become seriously hurt, hurt others, or die in the process of doing so. I want you to use your own better judgement here with that type of fear.

The fear we are focusing on and talking about here is the type of fear that keeps an old paradigm alive by trying to prevent you from creating a change, a new life for yourself. That's often where fear of failure is presented, or even the fear of success. The excuses and reasons are different for everyone, but the premise remains the same. Fear is preventing you from creating something more for yourself, from initiating the change you know you so desperately need and want to have.

CHANGE IS TOUGH!

You often hear about how people do not like change. I find from the work I do, that it's not about the changing that people don't like, it's that they don't like being forced to change. That's why when you make any major life changing decisions for yourself, you're bound to be met with opposition from those closest to you.

Why is that? Well it's because with your change, you are ultimately forcing a domino effect of change on someone else, often those closest to you.

Those who love you will almost always have your best intentions at heart and will want to see you succeed, but what they won't want is that effect it has on themselves. This type of change might include you moving away, further from those you love which creates a change in their lives because you're no longer a regular routine in it. Rest assured, we are creatures of habit and routine so when that is interrupted, uneasy feelings begin to surface.

When you get opposition to your new goals and plans which involve changing old routines and habits, it's important to understand that the opposition comes from others not wanting to deal with how it forces a change within their own lives as a result, no matter how small the perceived impact might be.

FALSE ENVIRONMENT APPEARING REAL

Let's dive a little bit into the actual fear emotion here elicited by change and see what this emotion really is, as well how you can use it to help you move into your goals, not pushing you away from them.

First, I want to get something very clear with you about the emotion of fear. Fear is a dream killer for most, but when you understand what fear means, where it comes from and why, then you can utilize it to know you're on the right track.

Let's break the word "fear" down into an acronym that I use all the time with my clients, and am absolutely in love with:

False
Environment
Appearing
Real

Repeat that again to yourself:

False Environment Appearing Real. So, what does this mean?

Well, let's think about this for a minute. Remember before when I was telling you that your subconscious mind cannot tell the difference between if something is real or imagined, and I gave you the example of the lemon? Well, that's essentially what the fear acronym is talking about.

The false environment appearing real is your subconscious mind believing that all those scary thoughts of failure and not knowing what you're doing, is happening right now. So, the emotions of feeling overwhelmed or like you are way over your head, begin to take over. You consciously become overwhelmed by those emotions, and make different conscious decisions and choices based on a perceived imagined reality that hasn't even happened yet. THAT my friend, is why people do not make big power moves to better their careers and therefore, their lives. This keeps people stuck in what they're doing, repeating the same results over and over.

Now, if you see fear for what it really is, imagined reality of something negative happening when it hasn't, then you can begin to steer those thoughts that are feeding that emotion over to things that make you feel excited and anticipatory towards your amazing big audacious goal.

INTERNAL NOTIFICATION SYSTEM

Can you eliminate that fear all together? Well, in some cases I guess you could but in most other cases, no. The fear emotion is a good thing if you use it as a notification of growth.

Here is what I mean by notification of growth and how you can use fear as a wonderful indicator that you are on the right track.

Remember earlier when we were talking about paradigms and how they control over 95% of our actions we take, and thus the results we get in our lives? Well, often when we begin to make changes that are in contradiction to a set paradigm we have around that specific topic, like opening your own business, the fear emotion is amplified, because it's the old limiting paradigm trying to remain in control and trying to stay alive.

Your paradigm will elicit thoughts within your conscious mind that will create the emotion of fear, which then creates more negative thoughts of failure of not being good enough, which ultimately slides you right back into repeating the same results that you are trying to move away from. The old paradigm wins, and you stay where you are.

When you begin to see fear for being a convincing argument that your old paradigm is using against you to prevent you from changing, then you must consciously choose to move through that fear feeling and do what you set out to do anyway. Move forward with trusting that all the answers and resources you need will appear for you once you make that self-empowering decision to go after your goal. Then and only then will you truly begin to grow and succeed.

Earl Nightingale once said, "Success is the progressive realization of a worthy ideal." So, if you are moving forward, progressively building your dreams and your goals, then you are already successful.

You are only a failure when you let your old limiting paradigm convince you through the fear emotion that you cannot do it, and then you stop trying.

I can promise you that if you move through those old negative thinking patterns you have about yourself that tell you you're not smart enough, not good enough, or whatever that internal dialogue is telling you, you will grow into a place within yourself you didn't even know existed. You will literally astound yourself!

INTERRUPTING THE OLD STORY

Each time you have a negative thought about your goal that is creating that intense and all so familiar fear emotion which prevents you from making that change, you must immediately become conscious of it. You must remember what the fear really is and what it means, and then interrupt that thought with a positive opposing statement.

Creating an opposing statement to what that fear dialogue is telling you is easy. For example, your fear is saying, "It's going to cost me way too much money and I'm going to fail if I try this." Pause, then become aware of that dialogue and what it's telling you. Write it all out on a piece of paper in detail, then on a new piece of paper write the opposite to what you wrote on the first paper.

"I have complete trust that the money I need will come to me in expected and unexpected ways that will support me through this exciting endeavor. I am already a success because I am working towards it. If others can do it, so can I."

Before I made the scary move to start my massage therapy practice, I had a mental paradigm that told me I wasn't smart enough and I would fall on my face if I tried. I would allow this internal dialogue to form who I was regarding reaching this goal, and it would determine the actions I would take toward it.

Which, in this case was none because that fear belief and negative dialogue inside my mind kept me from deciding to make that leap, the very same decision which propelled me into freedom and fulfillment in my massage career.

Once I was able to identify what was stopping me from making the choice to become my own boss, I reinforced that decision with positive self talk and things that would motivate me while I was on that path. Anything else that came into my conscious awareness that was not serving me and was trying to push me off that journey, I would immediately replace with the opposite.

Remember this my new friend, a paradigm is a belief you embody which has habits connected to it that physically acts out that belief, and a belief is simply something you tell yourself, or have been told, over and over.

Replace the negative thinking as soon as it pops up into your conscious awareness with the opposite of the fear dialogue, and you will find that eventually, you will weaken that paradigm so much so that your new positive replacement thoughts will now become the dominant directing force in your mind.

The repetitive nature of doing this mental task and mental conditioning is what will completely change your outcomes to where you're wanting to go. You will find that because you are consciously steering your thoughts and emotions to where you want them to go, you automatically begin to reflect that through your behaviors and actions. You will start attracting the right people, being in the right places, and attracting the right circumstances directly into your experience which quickly brings you closer to your big audacious goal.

"Two of the most powerful words you can ever utter are the words –

I am."

CHAPTER 8

Self-Image

***What does the successful YOU look, feel,
and act like, and how to bring this part
of you to the surface.***

Everything you have and are in life is a complete by-product of your habitual thoughts, learned behaviors and experiences up to this point, whether you agree with me or not. You are the person you believe yourself to be and you can never outgrow the limitations you place on yourself. You cannot outdo your current self-image, but the good news here is that you can learn to embody a new self-image.

THE PUMPKIN JAR

I once heard a recording of Earl Nightingale talking about a Wisconsin farmer walking through his field one day, stumbling over an empty glass jar in his pumpkin patch. The curious farmer decided to take a very small growing pumpkin and he poked it through the neck of the jar to the inside, being careful not the damage the pumpkin. He then rested it back on the ground and walked away.

Harvesting season arrived and the farmer went back to his pumpkin patch and worked his way down the rows of big ripe pumpkins, when he again came upon the glass jar, which he previously put the small growing pumpkin inside. The young pumpkin had completely filled its glass prison and having no more room, it stopped growing. The farmer broke the glass jar and held in his hand a runt pumpkin, which was half the size of all the other pumpkins and the exact shape of the jar.

Even though you aren't a pumpkin, your self-image is something like that jar. It shapes and determines the kind of person that you become. You can enlarge your self-image to allow yourself to grow through the same way that you created those self limitations in the first place; your experiences. The mental picture you have of yourself was developed through the events you went through, especially in your younger years as we have previously discussed. So, if you want to change your self-image but the experiences aren't currently physically available to you that could shape you into who you're wanting to be, you can do this synthetically through something called "imagined reality."

HOW YOUR IMAGINATION CREATES YOUR OUTCOMES

I mentioned several times now that our subconscious mind doesn't know if something it's experiencing is real or imagined.

Well, that means that you can use your imagination to trick your subconscious into thinking it's having an actual experience, which ultimately shapes how you're perceiving yourself and the world around you.

Worry is a good example of how you might create from a place that is from a synthetic experience. When you worry, you place yourself emotionally, mentally and even physically into an experience that hasn't even happened yet. You experienced that imaged reality like it was really happening to you right now.

If you're worrying about finances and placing yourself into imagined scenarios of financial failure, the emotional and physical reactions are identical to when you would experience that failure in real time. You feel nauseous, get a stiff neck, headaches and dizziness which are along the same lines of what you would physically feel if it was indeed happening to you in that moment.

As far as your subconscious mind and body are concerned, you have already failed. If you focus on that often and repeat that cycle of worry enough, you will create that to be your actual reality.

You can use this information now to your advantage, knowing that you can consciously choose to feed your mind a synthetic imagined reality experience to one that feels ease and flow. A great way to do this, which I often employ on myself, is to remember a time in your life where you felt like you succeeded at something. Maybe it was mastering learning an instrument or finally receiving a certification for something you worked hard for.

Do you remember how proud you were? Do you remember how excited you felt? You were on top of the world and all you wanted to do was tell others and think about how awesome it went for you.

Now, bring up those feelings and attach them to the thought of succeeding with your goal you determined for yourself within your business. Sit in that thought even if it's only for a couple of minutes, and really feel those emotions when you think about finally reaching your goal. See yourself in this image and the look on your face, the posture your body is in and the confidence you exude to others. Now, use your imagination and step into that "future you" and see what they are seeing through their eyes.

Doing this type of positive self-imagery is the exact opposite of worrying and will surely begin priming your subconscious mind to act out that experience to create it into your current reality.

THE SELF-IMAGE PARADIGM

Anything that you're going to do and work towards accomplishing is dependent on your self-image. Your self-image is going to determine if you fail or succeed with your goal. You can consciously know you're wanting to do something, but the paradigm that is attached to how you view yourself within that goal is what will either push you off the path you're trying to get on or create an easier flow to that path.

You see, you can tell yourself that you want to be a certain way and be a specific type of person, but what happens is that you will begin to feel frustrated because you are still having the same thoughts and reactions to what's going on around you. Nothing seems to be changing, even though you want it to.

Like all paradigms, the self-image paradigm you embody is on a set course and has a set program to uphold. Do you notice people who have a negative self-image when it comes to how their body looks, they tend to yo-yo with their results? Why is that? Why is it that when they make the decision to either lose weight or gain more muscle, even though they diet and work hard at the gym, they suddenly fall off the band wagon and go right back to where they were before?

Well, it all has to do with the fact that they haven't re-programmed their paradigm which determines how they subconsciously see themselves.

The self-image paradigm is referred to by Maxwell Maltz as a "psycho-cybernetic mechanism" in his book *Psycho-Cybernetics*. Think of an airplane on autopilot flying from point A to point B. The airplane is always being knocked off course due to turbulence and other factors, but the cybernetic mechanism which is the set course destination of the autopilot, will detect the variance that it has gone off course, and make the appropriate adjustments to get it right back on track.

Your self-image paradigm works in exactly the same way. It has a set program on autopilot that detects the change and does everything it can to get it back on that course to the current programming. That is why when people try to make big changes to themselves, the results are usually small and temporary. You cannot change the behavior without changing the paradigm first, as it will always revert back to its dominant program currently running.

So, what are your beliefs about your own success? Do you have a self-image that is telling you that you cannot own your own business, as you're not an entrepreneur? Does your current self-image tell you that you're too financially strapped, or bad things always happen to you? What about the old cultural belief we tend to adopt from our parents that tell us we must work really hard long hours to make good money?

These are all programmed beliefs that make up our self-image and these beliefs can all be changed easily with dedication, study and persistence. It's impossible for you to not make those changes on your own self-image now that you understand this information, and the way to make those changes is the same way you would change any mental programming; through study of the mind and the repetitive use of imagined reality to teach your subconscious mind how you want it to be. Repetition here is the absolute key to any change you want to embody.

FUTURE SELF-PROFILE TECHNIQUE

There is an amazing and powerful technique I have my students do whenever I'm working with them on creating a new self-image, called *The Future Self-Profile*. It will prompt you to analyze and feel into the type of entrepreneur you want to become, while helping you identify and eliminate old limiting self-image patterns. It's discussed in much more detail within my *Massage Therapist Success Fundamentals* program, but for the sake of this book, the premise is to imagine yourself becoming the person who has already reached your goal. Then we work on breaking down those attributes to create your synthetic reality, tricking your subconscious mind into thinking it's who you are becoming now.

When you have a clearer image of the person who you want to become within your practice, start writing a letter to the present you from that future you. What does that future you want to say to you about reaching your goal? What advice does your future you have for you?

This is a great subconscious association technique you can use to elicit some fantastic emotions and ideas around where you're headed. I call this mind-hack exercise 'Letter from your future self.'

When you do this type of exercise, you want to tap into what future you as the business owner entrepreneur behaves and acts like. This is like creating an updated version of yourself, an avatar of yourself if you may. Being specific is okay and recommended amongst many personal growth experts, however, I want to caution about where that specificity is coming from. Is it coming from your ego, fear, or limiting paradigm? Or is it coming from a place of authenticity and service?

When you create out of ego and if it doesn't shape exactly how you want, not necessarily what you need, you set yourself up for negatively connected emotions, which shuts down the positive creative process and leaves you in a confusing loop of unwanted events to show up in your experience.

The repetitive unwanted events are usually signs that you're emotionally invested in a negative thought or idea. They're like your engine warning light when you need to get your vehicle serviced; but the difference here is that it's not as easy as an engine light. It is important to practice being consciously aware of your own thoughts and to be able to analyse the events from that place of mindfulness to your situations. This can be accomplished through meditation and self awareness exercises, which I recommend to my students as a supplement to my program.

I AM

Two of the most powerful words you can ever utter are the words "I am." These two simple words are programming your self-image every single time you say it. So, going forward, I want you to become consciously aware when you attach these words to any sentence, even in a joking way. Then, use those two words to consciously affirm the type of person you want to become with your exciting new goal, and the type of life you want to have.

Often, I would focus on something that I want to embody within myself. Let's take writing this book for example. Months before I even wrote this book or knew who I was writing it for, I would write down a dozen or so general "I am" statements and record them into a simple voice recorder app on my cell phone.

"I am an accomplished and successful author."

"I am creating an abundant and prosperous life."

"I am confident in my ability to share my knowledge."

"I am becoming clearer with my goal and what I want to achieve every day."

"I am becoming more aware every day of who I am meant to serve with my information."

"I am grateful for the ability to clearly flow my words onto paper easily and effortlessly."

"I am helping thousands of people all over the world understand their true greatness."

These are just a sample of what I would record with my own voice into the recorder app on my mobile phone. Once I was happy with the tone and clarity in my voice, the headphones would go in and I would go workout with it playing on repeat. I would listen to it in the vehicle when driving alone, while walking my dogs every night, while cleaning my house, and even while I slept.

I noticed a big difference in how I was feeling and acting within several weeks of doing this consistently, and the great thing is that it takes nearly no effort at all to put your headphones in your ears, press play on your phone, and slide it into your pocket while you do mundane activities anyways. When I slept, I would have it play very low in the background as to not disturb me.

Once I started noticing that what I had been affirming to myself was becoming my reality and what I was beginning to act out in my daily activities, I would move onto the next thing that I wanted to work on with myself. You can do this with anything from fitness, health, relationships, business... absolutely anything. The interesting part about embodying these affirmations is that it happens so subtly, you don't even notice it until you consciously become aware of it by looking at the changes.

The reason why the changes feel so subtle is because YOU ARE that now. It becomes a program and it becomes a subconscious normality for you to behave and act in ways now that are congruent with the repetitive autosuggestions you were giving yourself.

Figure out what you want to change and understand your current internal dialogue around that topic. Then shift it to a new dialogue which embodies what it is your really want to accomplish and before you know it, you will find it becomes your natural state to think and feel that way.

"IDENTIFYING YOUR IDEAL CLIENT'S SITUATION AND HOW YOU CAN HELP THEM, GIVES CLEAR INSTRUCTIONS FOR YOUR SUBCONSCIOUS MIND TO BEGIN TO ALIGN YOU PHYSICALLY WITH THE RIGHT PEOPLE, PLACES, AND OPPORTUNITIES TO ATTRACT THOSE IDEAL CLIENTS RIGHT INTO YOUR BUSINESS AND ON YOUR MASSAGE TABLE."

CHAPTER 9

Your Business Niche & Ideal Client

***Identifying your business niche and
ideal client to help your business
to thrive, not just survive.***

For me, the coolest thing about what I teach massage therapists is showing them something that they often overlook,
and that is the power of specificity.

I was in love with those "choose your own adventure" books
when I was younger. The reason why I loved them so much was
because I was empowered and enabled with the option to change
the outcome of the character's destiny, whichever way was presented to me. It taught me as well a valuable lesson regarding
the law of cause and effect, in the sense that our behaviors and

actions have an equal and opposite reaction from our environment. The thoughts you place into your subconscious, which show up as a vibration of energy, are translated through your emotions and your actions.

Everything has a match and compatibility, a bit like a lock and key.

If you place negative scenarios and outcomes into the reality you imagine, you will find yourself automatically aligning with those circumstances and situations in your life that match that vibration. It is just how it works as it is a universal law called the 'Law of Attraction', just like the law of gravity is always working whether you understand it or not. It doesn't take a break just so you can analyze it and decide if it's something you want to have or not.

When choosing your own adventure with your audacious goal of creating your own business and being your own boss, one of the most liberating and impactful things you will begin to understand in all of this, is that you can choose your clients. Yes, you can choose the types of clients that are a match for the product or service you are delivering, and which will make the biggest impact on the success of your business.

You learned a lot about self-image in the last chapter and how that self-image can really determine if you will fail or succeed in any endeavour. Well, there is a client image that I am going to help you understand and utilize to your benefit as well.

WHY IS CHOOSING YOUR IDEAL CLIENT IMPORTANT?

Well, because you are going to want to attract to you the type of client that is going to be a match for the type of business you want, the type of services you have, and more importantly a problem you can solve for someone who is looking for a solution.

When I was a practicing massage therapist, I worked on anyone and everyone who wanted to book an appointment with me. I worked on pregnant women, post injury motor vehicle incident claims, to just a Swedish relaxation massage. I never homed in on an ideal client, and I just tried to make a client out of anyone and everyone. While this strategy (or lack of it) seemed to work OK, it probably took me 5x longer to get the amount of quality clients as I would have if I understood the ideal client principle that I'm showing you.

Without being conscious of it at the time, I in fact did have an ideal client but I didn't know it. I was able to solve a problem that not a lot of other massage therapists at the time were able to solve; I had the skill and knowledge of relieving and reversing the symptoms of carpal tunnel. If I understood this principle of an establishing ideal client, I would have marketed my services to these clients who were suffering from this issue who wanted to avoid surgery. I can guarantee that I would have easily attracted quality clients because I could solve a problem they had, because they were also looking for me. Not only that, but it also made competition irrelevant as no one was focusing specifically on this problem that I was solving.

Some very important mentors in my life helped me understand this principle. Now as a business success & mindset coach, I am utilizing the power of identifying an ideal client for my own practice, which is helping massage therapists achieve success through bridging the gap between what they want and achieving it. This concept of choosing the type of client you want to serve is going to help you narrow down to your specific niche and expertise. I'm a huge advocate regarding becoming an expert at one thing, and decent at everything else.

You understand by now the importance of being very clear and detailed about your goal in the aspect of how it feels once you have accomplished it, what it looks like, who's in it, the amount of money you want to earn, and how many employees you want if any at all.

Well, the same goes for identifying your ideal client, which you will want to determine as quickly as possible for clarity of your goal. This might change your goal a little bit too, which is totally okay. If your goal shifts and morphs slightly from finding out what type of clients you want to serve and why, then you're growing it and adding to it. You're also growing and adding to yourself things that maybe you didn't allow yourself to recognize before or maybe you are uncovering a hidden desire regarding your career path within this industry. The primary purpose of a goal is to grow, remember?

SPECIFICITY IS KEY

As mentioned, if I was given this information back then when I ran my massage therapy business, I would have without a doubt narrowed down to working with clients who suffer from Carpal Tunnel Syndrome due to repetitive use. My ideal client would have been more in the chronic stage of the condition and entertaining at surgery as their next option; however, they were directed to try massage therapy to relieve the tightness and tension in the forearm. See how specific this is?

Why would I have chosen this for myself? Well, because I had a good understanding of how to correct Carpal Tunnel Syndrome without having to go under the knife. I understood the anatomy and physiology of this topic and explained it well to my clients. I was able to help many people find amazing relief from their symptoms if they stuck with the preventative routine, I gave them.

When you decide on what you have a knack and interest for within this career and you can specialize in it, then YOU can decide who is your ideal client. You become clear on their frustrations from where they are at and the best outcomes in their mind to what their problem is. Often, what your client thinks is their problem and best outcome isn't always accurate. You are the expert so that's where your services come into play, because you can serve that client and give them the answers they need to their specific problem better than anyone else. This is what sets you apart and makes so called "competition" practically irrelevant. When you truly get this concept, it makes the idea of competition extremely insignificant.

As you determine and understand who your ideal client is, you are now better able to tailor your marketing to attract those specific potential clients. Does that mean you're not going to take other clients? No, not at all! It just means that you have a focused niche which allows you to find your clients much easier, because they're looking for you too.

YOUR MODALITY IS NOT YOUR NICHE

It's a very common mistake for massage therapists to think that things like trigger point therapy, active release technique, cupping, paraffin therapy, aromatherapy, chair massage, etc., is a niche when it's not. These are modalities, not niches. To put it in another way, a niche is a focused approach on a specific market need. This means that your client has a specific problem which you can help them solve as the specialist in that area.

Examples of a niche are things like chronic pain, post surgery, office ergonomics, whiplash, disabilities, geriatric specific, prenatal, postpartum, or carpal tunnel syndrome as mentioned earlier.

BEING SPECIFIC CAN BE SCARY

A mentor of mine, named Angela, told me once that if I ever wanted to become universal with my services, I first had to learn to become very specific. Those words made such complete sense to me, and absolutely changed the way I saw niches, and how I operate my own business today. In your massage therapy profession, you can work with almost anyone and help them. But, because that is such a broad and expansive energy and not focused at all, you will get a mixed bag of mixed results. Sometimes you will have a good month of business, sometimes a very bad month of business. However, now that you have the understanding to become clear and focused on the type of individual you are serving, and the niche you're focusing on, not only are your results going to start matching your desires, you will also be creating more clients because if it.

One of the scariest things for an entrepreneur is being so specific with something, that you isolate others from finding you because of it. I'm going to challenge that limiting thought and get you to look at it this way. Identifying your ideal client's situation and how you can help them, gives clear instructions for your subconscious mind to begin to align you physically with the right people, places, and opportunities to attract those ideal clients right into your business and on your massage table.

Don't kid yourself, your clients are looking for you just as much as you are looking for them. These clients that you are focusing on are going to be telling their friends and family all about you and the phone is going to be ringing off the hook with inquiries asking you to help them with their specific problem, even if it isn't your specific focused niche.

This is how you become universal with your services by becoming very specific with who you serve and why.

Now, ask yourself the right questions to get started and let the ideas flow from there.

What makes you unique?

Who are you wanting to serve?

What is your ideal client's specific problem?

How does your ideal client describe their problem in THEIR words?

What is your ideal client's desired outcome to their problem?

How does your ideal client describe their desired outcomes in THEIR words?

What story do you want your ideal client to tell others after your service?

Remember, be specific and be clear and ask yourself empowering questions so that you can find out exactly who you want to be and the type of client you want to work with. If you sit down and decide to create an image of your ideal client, then through that mental clarity, you will find that all the resources and information you need will begin to appear into your experience in no time.

"IF YOU BELIEVE THAT THERE IS AN ABUNDANCE OF CLIENTS IN YOUR EXPERIENCE, THEN YOUR SUBCONSCIOUS MIND WILL ALIGN YOU WITH THE RIGHT IDEAS, INSPIRATIONS, PEOPLE, AND SITUATIONS THAT CONTINUE TO GIVE YOU THAT ABUNDANCE MINDSET."

CHAPTER 10

Success Through Service

What you put out is what you will get back in return. Understand how leaving those you encounter with more than they came to you with, will create even more abundance in your business and your life.

I have mentioned a few times the value of being of service to others. But I didn't really elaborate on why the mentality of service is not only important to the success of your business, but to your success in almost every other area of your life as well.

I'm assuming you likely grew up like I did with the mentality of competition. We learned as children and young adults about healthy competition, and while I do believe there is such a thing as healthy competition like sports or games in general, it often bleeds over into our adulthood, especially into business.

Competition in business isn't something that I believe in myself, and I understand that a lot of business professionals will scoff at that comment. But I'll tell you why I see it that way. I believe that the competition mentality in business creates and feeds a negative paradigm a lot of people have, which is that there is a lack of abundance in this world. It's a paradigm that tells you that if you don't put your competitor out of business, then they will steal all your clients and put you out of business.

The ironic thing here is that because it's a subconscious program to think this way, that paradigm will create your experience to be exactly like that for you. That is the wonderful thing about the subconscious mind, it doesn't understand if something is good or bad for you, it just goes by the programming it has.

So, if you feel there is a lack in this world, there will be a lack in this world for you. On the contrary if you believe that there is an abundance of clients in your experience, then your subconscious mind will align you with the right ideas, inspirations, people and situations that continue to give you that abundance mindset.

WHAT YOU PUT OUT IS WHAT COMES BACK TO YOU

It is quite mind boggling how much in control we are of our outcomes, when we don't even know it. It's the simple belief that there is not enough, so you have to fight and compete for these limited resources. This will set the scenarios in your life to occur in that manner, to validate that paradigm.

So, this takes me now to how important being of service to others is. When I talk about being of service to others, I'm not just talking about giving massages or implementation of other healing techniques. What I am referring to is the giving and receiving of abundance in all areas of your life. What you put out is what comes back to you. It doesn't matter what anyone else is doing, as you want to make sure that you are being the best and most effective person you can be. You want to do things in a certain way and be aware of how you treat others in a way which leaves them with the experience of increase, so that you can begin to form and create what you want coming back to you in return.

As I've discussed before, what you think controls your emotions, and your emotions control the vibration your body is in. Your vibration determines your behaviors and actions, and your actions are responsible for the reaction you get from your environment, an environment that you play a very large role in. That action and reaction dance is responsible for the results you get in your life. So, when you're in alignment with what you really want and focused on being of service to others, your results will be very positive. When you're not, your results will be negative or much less than you desire.

Showing others that you are genuinely interested in the betterment and success of others, opens the door for you to not only become kinder to yourself, but it also energetically goes out into the universe for that phenomenal vibration to come back to you in the form of kindness and cooperation from others. It's an energetic relationship of cause and effect. You don't receive abundance by doing certain things, you receive abundance by doing things a certain way!

When you see the best in others, you're going to be in a great mood and vibration most of the time, and even when bad things happen, which they will, you will be able to respond to negative situations versus reacting to them.

It is important to know that energy returns to its source. So, if you give, you shall receive. You can practice incorporating this into your way of thinking every single day, in everything you do and everyone you meet. If you do this, you will most definitely have a richer, more abundant life.

SHIFTING YOUR PERCEPTION

I can have a big personality sometimes, and I can also be quite opinionated, which in the past opened the doors for a lot of disagreements with others and some hard feelings. During that time, I wasn't aware of these types of concepts and the idea of treating everyone in my life like they were someone I could learn from in some way.

It reminds me of a time when I had a strained relationship with someone I worked with, we just weren't getting along and were disagreeing on most things. It came to the point where I didn't enjoy going into work each day, as I was starting to expect minor confrontations. To make matters worse, this person at the time was my boss.

A wise friend of mine gave me a suggestion to shift my perception and see what came back to me in return. So, I remembered a technique that a colleague of mine used on one of her clients who was having marital problems with her partner. She was asked to make a list each day of 10 positive qualities her partner possessed that she could identify each day for two weeks. After a week of doing this, her client noticed huge improvements with how they interacted.

So, I decided that I would do the exact same thing. I scheduled myself each morning to go into work 15-minutes earlier, before my boss came in, and write out a list of 10 things I liked about him. Well, I'll tell you, the first couple days of doing this I struggled. My mind was automatically associating him with negative aspects, so shifting over to positive felt very uncomfortable. It was easy for me to think negatively about him because I practiced it so much. My negative paradigm was trying to get in the way. But I persisted and decided that having a harmonious relationship with him was a much better option than otherwise.

After a couple of days, the list of positive attributes became a bit longer and longer. By the end of that first week, I was easily writing down 10 to 15 aspects I enjoyed about him. I wrote things such as how I enjoyed his humor when he was in a good mood, or that I felt he was very good at negotiating with others. By the second week, I noticed a shift in how we were interacting. It was almost like I was only in his company when things were calm, or when he was in a good mood. Our discussions turned from that of disagreeing on everything, to talking about things we were either both neutral on or things that we agreed on.

What the heck was happening?! What is the logical explanation to why this practice of identifying and focusing on the positive about someone, works so well in creating harmonious relationships? I figured out that it all comes down to perception.

When you perceive and have a belief that something is a certain way for you, or that certain people treat you in certain ways, your subconscious mind looks for situations to validate that belief. And, because we think thoughts that are in harmony with our paradigms, our perception on how things are is going to determine how we interpret our interactions, and even the type of interactions we find ourselves in.

VALUE OF INCREASE

So, for everyone you interact with, leave them with the value of increase. Give to them something that they didn't have before your interaction with them. This can even be as simple as a genuine compliment or smile from across the room. These are actions that produce positive results from your environment, and it also does something for you on a deeper level when you leave someone feeling good.

If you find yourself having a particular issue with someone in your life, think about the story I shared with you here. As much as your paradigm will push you to act differently, I encourage you to start programming the solution into your subconscious mind. Ask yourself the following questions:

What about this person do I admire?
How does this person add value to my life?
What do I see in this person that is good?
What aspects of this person reminds me of someone I enjoy?
What value can I give to this person?

SET YOUR CONSCIOUS INTENT EACH DAY

Make up your mind that regardless of what has happened to you in the past, you are going to do something amazing in the future. Each morning when you wake up, tell yourself "Today, I'm going to see things differently than I have seen them before. I am going to look for aspects of my day that make me feel good and I am going to look for things in others that I admire, even if they are small things."

That conscious intent will set you up for better, more productive paradigms that are in complete alignment with what you want and what you're working towards. Be aware throughout the day of what is happening around you. Do not let other people or situations determine which way your thoughts are directed and stay on course with your intention. Think great thoughts about your current job, your current company, the people in your life and the path that you are currently on.

This will take a bit of practice and self-awareness building on your part, but the more you do it, the more in control you will feel and the easier it will get. Then you will notice how things for you will begin to flow with ease and harmony, and when those bumps in the road occur, you will start to become aware of how easily and quickly you move past them.

"THERE IS SOMETHING VERY POWERFUL ABOUT WORKING IN A GROUP TOWARDS A COMMON GOAL WHERE EVERYONE IS CONTRIBUTING TO ONE ANOTHER IN ORDER TO HELP EACH OTHER FLOURISH AND SUCCEED."

CHAPTER 11

The Power of Many

Understand the power of the Mastermind Principle, and how to make it work for you in your business.

I wanted to dedicate an entire chapter to this very important principle in business that is so often misunderstood, and even sometimes overlooked entirely by new entrepreneurs. If you have never heard of what I am about to explain to you, then I strongly encourage you to go over this chapter several times. I want you to have a true understanding of how working with a mastermind group will take your business places that you might have never been able to take it on your own.

I first became aware of the mastermind principle a few years ago when I read the book, *Think and Grow Rich* by Napoleon Hill. Then, a short time later this principle surfaced again in my awareness when I started working with my colleague Bob Proctor who I've mentioned previously, and who you might remember from the 2006 movie documentary *The Secret.*

I incorporate this principle now into my own business and it has proven its weight in gold. Not only have I added to other business owner's successes, I have had my own results multiplied by those contributing to mine. I have brought up the topics regarding things that I'm trying to accomplish in my career, and suddenly I have multiple brains contributing to ideas that I might not have previously come up with on my own.

THE MASTERMIND PRINCIPLE

The Mastermind Principle was first made popular by the previously mentioned Napoleon Hill's book called *Think and Grow Rich,* published in 1937, as it showcased one of America's most wealthy businessmen, named Andrew Carnegie. Mr. Carnegie started with absolutely nothing when he arrived in America from Scotland in 1848. Fast forward a half-century later, he was the richest man in the country after helping build the American steel industry.

Napoleon Hill interviewed and worked closely with Mr. Carnegie while writing *Think and Grow Rich,* and he was given the knowledge of the Mastermind Principle. In fact, Mr. Carnegie credits all his riches to this principle.

Hill defines the mastermind principle as, "Coordination of knowledge and effort, in a spirit of harmony, between two or more people, for the attainment of a definite purpose." In simpler terms, it means surrounding yourself with talented people who share your goals. The reason being is that the alignment of several intelligent and creative minds is immensely more powerful than just one.

This principle has two sides to it. One is economic in nature, and the other is energetic/mental.

The economic side is more obvious. Heeding the advice of other intelligent individuals, who want to help you, will place you in a much stronger economic advantage.

"This form of cooperative alliance has been the basis of nearly every great fortune," Hill writes. "Your understanding of this great truth may definitely determine your financial status."

The energetic/mental part is more abstract, but extremely important to grasp.

"No two minds ever come together without, thereby, creating a third, invisible, intangible force which may be likened to a third mind," explains Hill.

Hill compares the human brain to a battery. A group of batteries create more energy and power than just one battery. So, a group of minds together will create more energy of thought than just one mind.

Each of these minds brings something different to the table, which can give you ideas and inspirations about your own practice that you might not have previously come to on your own.

One of my favorite quotes by Napoleon Hill is this:

"Analyze the record of any man who has accumulated a great fortune, and many of those who have accumulated modest fortunes, and you will find that they have either consciously, or unconsciously employed the mastermind principle."

I spoke earlier about the difference between a "conscious competent" and an "unconscious competent," and this is a great example of how we can unconsciously do the right things. It's almost as if there is a universal source or energy guiding us to intuitively have the right ideas and to take the right actions. However, the difference is that when you're consciously doing it, you understand why you're doing it and can make conscious choices to better yourself and others from that place of knowledge.

WHY I COACH THIS PRINCIPLE TO MY OWN STUDENTS

When I work with my students in group programs, which is 95% of my business, I automatically incorporate The Mastermind Principle into their program. There is something so powerful about working in groups towards a common goal, where everyone is contributing to one another in order to help another flourish and succeed.

A mastermind group needs to be a well-oiled machine for it to work. So, that means participants need to be dedicated to regular gatherings which will be agreed upon by everyone in the group. I have seen mastermind groups meet once per week, or even once per month and sometimes longer in-between. I recommend that a once per month agreed on time to meet is often most effective, as the group members can plan their schedules in advance to ensure their attendance.

The group works best with around 4 to 8 people, and no more than 10 because of the constraints of time. Also, for this reason, a planned agenda should be part of the regular routine for your mastermind group. If you are in different cities, it's very easy to plan a conference call and there are plenty of free online services that will offer multiple options to accomplish this.

There are a set of mastermind principles I teach to my students and have them read out at the beginning of each call. This is of such importance as part of the meeting because it sets the stage for the intent around the group. As well, it programs your subconscious mind which creates a positive group paradigm. Businesses and corporations often call this group paradigm a "corporate culture."

Each member should be supported and encouraged by the others. It's important for this to not be taken lightly, as we have discussed previously about leaving others with the impression of increase. The principle is that we can believe for others what they might not be able to fully believe for themselves. You can give much better encouragement and advice when you're not wrapped up emotionally in the problem or obstacle being presented by another member that they are seeking to solve.

A mastermind group should always be run like a serious and proper meeting as this isn't a social club gathering. This is about helping yourself and each other grow to expand into the brilliant entrepreneurs you all are. So, this means that the set rules are followed, intentions are made clear and the direction of the meeting stays on track and on time.

USE THE MASTERMIND PRINCIPLE IN ALL AREAS OF YOUR LIFE

You can most definitely create your own mastermind group however you wish. What I presented above are just some of the guidelines that I follow and work within my own business, and what I recommend for my students to follow. If you wanted to have a free for all within your meetings, instead of following a set agenda and time limits, fill your boots! Will it be as effective? Well, I do not believe that there are always right or wrong ways to accomplish the same task in this case, only more or less effective. It all depends on your willingness to grow and your ability to make decisions based on other member's advice, which could lead to some very positive and lucrative changes.

If you are starting your own business, especially if you are a solo entrepreneur in this endeavour, then I cannot encourage you enough to start networking. Find yourself a set of like-minded, goal orientated entrepreneurs to form a powerful and very beneficial mastermind group. Doing this will set you up to be able to collaborate with people who have solutions to the obstacles that you might face within your practice. Your mastermind group can help you with your own marketing, business ideas and advice around your specific niche.

You will find when you incorporate this principle into your work and even personal life, that not only will you fast track your way to success, but you will create an avenue for solutions that will provide more growth for yourself than you ever thought was possible.

"It's called growth for a reason because it doesn't come instantly. It takes a lot of repetition, and a lot of study to truly allow the information you learn to absorb into your subconscious mind, so it can start to grow."

CHAPTER 12

How to Succeed

It's easy to become derailed, but it is just as easy to succeed if you stick with it.

One of the most liberating moments I have ever been through was when I truly understood that my reality was mine to create. The more I studied and became a sponge for this material that I am now teaching you, the more I understood that life doesn't just happen to us, it happens for us.

Everything you see around you from the TV in your home, to the business across the street, to the cell phone on your table, and this very book you're reading, came from someone's mind. Everything originates in your conscious mind before it's created into the physical world.

Bob Proctor often says that before the Wright brothers who were just a couple of bicycle mechanics took flight, which was the beginning of air travel, those around them told them they were crazy. They were told that people cannot fly, flying is for the birds. However, they had a goal, they had a burning desire that what they thought up in their minds, they were going to create into reality no matter what. They did exactly that because they believed in themselves and didn't let the "peanut gallery" outside of them influence what they could and couldn't do.

YOU CAN CREATE WHATEVER YOU TRULY DESIRE

You know, it doesn't matter who you are, where you came from or what type of life you had growing up, if you want to do something and can create a clear picture of it in your mind, I guarantee you that you can create it to form in your reality. If you can see it in your mind, you can hold it in your hand.

When I was in my late teens, I was told by someone I worked with that I might as well scratch lotto tickets for the rest of my life because I wouldn't amount to anything important. I wasn't very good in school; I had chronic poor grades and lacked any ambition or drive to do anything with myself. As I matured and began to figure out what type of life I wanted to have, it was always stuck in the back of my mind that because I didn't do very well in school, I probably wouldn't do very well in business either.

In my mid 20's, because of severe social anxiety, I embarked on a self-improvement journey, and began to study the mind and how what we think and feel, holds absolute dominion over the results we get in our lives. I started to apply much of what I was learning within my own life and found that things started turning around for me as I expanded my knowledge and understanding of myself. Fast forwarding now to over a decade later, which seemed to have happened in the blink of an eye, I have accomplished so much in my life because of this information. I have rubbed shoulders and worked with some extremely important and influential people, I had a successful massage therapy and clinical hypnotherapy practice; I've traveled to many places around the world, I have a phenomenal relationship with my partner, and I have a coaching business which has began to develop into something bigger than I could have imagined.

I now sit here in my chair writing these words to you about to finish my first of many books, reflecting back on my life and thinking to myself that if I believed that guy who told me I should scratch lotto tickets for the rest of my life, because he didn't believe I was capable of doing anything for myself, then maybe I would be somewhere entirely different than where I am today. I know I would be somewhere completely different, and probably a very different person too, if I didn't make the most important investment I've ever made, the investment in my personal and professional growth.

IT'S CALLED GROWTH FOR A REASON

Your own personal and professional growth comes down to a decision to learn about the mind, and how you play a larger part within this world. It's called growth for a reason because it doesn't come instantly. It takes much repetition and a lot of study to truly allow the information you learn to absorb into your subconscious mind, so it can start to grow into something even bigger than you imagined.

Things will come up for you in the process of shifting aware-ness that you're going through. You're going to be faced with some challenging beliefs and insecurities about yourself that you didn't even know existed, because you have never shone your light in this area before. Before this point, you were never fully aware of how in control you are of the results you get in your life.

You will be faced with self doubt, and the doubt from others. You will be faced with the fear of the unknown and the fear of failure. You will ask yourself if it's worth the pain and discomfort that you feel, to have the life you truly want. I believe it is worth it, because the pain and discomfort of not having what you want in your career, and life in general, will always be there if you don't aim for something more, something greater than what you're doing now. Those feelings of growth that are often not very pleasing, are also very temporary, and when you do reach your goal, I know you will say that you'd do it all over again.

The biggest obstacle for me was my impatience about the results I wanted to have, as I felt it wasn't happening quick enough. I would work on myself with meditation and conscious creation writing for weeks, and not see much happening. So, I would become hard on myself and say it's not working, and what's the point. I would then slide back into my old non-pro-ductive habits and routines, to live much of the same results I lived before because it was easy and familiar.

However, the more I learned about patience and that every-thing unfolds the way it's meant to, I turned from being impa-tient, to allowing. I focused on what I was happy about and what I already loved about my life and my career. When I did this and trusted the process, that's when I would notice things happening. I grew from having to go through these experiences and continue to do so, and I can understand how to better myself from them.

DON'T DIG UP THAT SEED

Picture your goal like a seed you plant in the earth. Before you plant that seed, you carefully look for a place where the soil is rich, and you ensure that it's a place that gets a lot of sunlight too. You go out and water this seed every single day, waiting for it to sprout because you understand that there is a process the seed needs to go through to transform into a plant.

You would not plant a seed, water it, then get angry and despondent the next day because you see that there is no sprout yet, then dig it up to see exactly why it hasn't grown into a full plant. That would be silly! But, for some reason people do this with their goals and their own self development. Your goal is that seed, and the constant practice and study you put into priming yourself for that goal each day, is the water to that seed.

You will want to dig up that seed sometimes, but don't. I promise you that if you hold patiently to your desired goal, and practice seeing it every single day in your mind, then you will achieve it. It must manifest, it's universal law that it does. The only time these goals do not come into fruition is when you kill them with fear and doubt.

I have seen people go from nothing to everything, all because they decided to take control of their results by thinking differently. Beware of falling into the trap of comparing yourself to others too, as every single person has their own speed and process of growth. What might come quickly and easily for someone else, could take much longer for you because you might have more resistance in that specific area. Some seeds grow quicker than others, the seed however always grows under the right conditions and when nurtured.

YOU'VE GOT THIS

I encourage you to read this material several times over, as you will see and understand things the second and third time that you didn't see the first time. This isn't because it wasn't there, it's because your awareness has shifted, so you are able to understand it better than you did before.

I have absolutely no doubt in my mind that you can reach your goal on your own if you heed my advice and the information in this book. However, even the most knowledgeable and successful entrepreneurs have mentors and coaches because these people are guides along your journey. The information in this book is pulled from my *Massage Therapist Success Fundamentals program*, which helps you with this personal growth process.

I spoke before about the power of working in groups, and when my students work with me, they not only get my direct support, but they also become part of an ongoing supportive group of other like-minded individuals who have gone through or are on a very similar journey.

The simple fact that you're reading this material now, shows that you are ready for something more than what you have and you're looking for assistance in getting there. It's my hope for you that you practice the information and exercises presented in this book and take that scary, yet exciting step towards creating the career and life you truly want.

"THE BIGGEST AND BEST INVESTMENT YOU CAN EVER MAKE IS ON YOUR OWN PERSONAL GROWTH AND DEVELOPMENT, AS IT'S A SKILL YOU CAN TRANSFER OVER TO THOSE YOU LOVE AND CARE ABOUT, AND THAT YOU CAN USE IN ANY AREA OF YOUR LIFE."

CHAPTER 13

Putting it All Together

Summary of the process.

How many times are you going to hope, dream and wish things were different for you without acting on those thoughts? At a minimum, what I want you to get out of this book is an awareness of yourself that you might not have gotten if you didn't pick up this material in the first place. At a maximum, it's my hope that you use this as an inspirational platform to leap from and create the life and career that you really want.

I want to summarize for you what I feel are the most important parts of what we have gone over in this book, so the information presented sticks within your mind. I hope you can begin the process of repetitive study to have your subconscious mind begin to incorporate this new awareness into new results.

I can promise you that you will begin to see things in a different perspective than you ever saw things before, which automatically will begin to change the way you feel and the way you act and therefore the results you get.

GOALS

Whether you drive a car or take public transit, you have a set destination you are going to within this world. I want you to think about your own goals this way as well. Your goal is like the coordinates you put into your GPS, so that you can physically begin moving towards that destination. Without those coordinates, you're just going to be wandering around aimlessly, not ever really having a destination in mind. So many people do this, and often this sets people up for mediocre experiences and ultimately a mediocre life. Repeating much of the same, over and over.

First and foremost, have yourself a clearly defined big audacious goal that is going to scare and excite you at the same time. Spending your time with things you have already done before, or a goal that you know you can do based on what your current environment yields to you isn't living, that's just existing. Write down your goal and look at it every day. Really feel what it would be like to have that manifested into your experience and become excited about it. Your goal might shift slightly and change a bit, but that's okay if it comes from a place of awareness to what you want, not out of fear.

Remember that the purpose of a goal is to grow, and the stuff you achieve on the other side of that goal is just the icing on the cake. Who you are once you have accomplished that goal will be a different person than who you are now; you will be a wiser more experienced YOU.

SUBCONSCIOUS PARADIGMS

Paradigms are another word for how you are programmed subconsciously, and each paradigm is made up of a multitude of habits. Somewhere around 95% of what we do in our waking state is habitual, so that means that most of our life is determined by the subconscious programming we have running at any given time.

Not all paradigms are negative, so don't mistakenly see the word 'paradigm' as a bad thing. A paradigm itself is just what it is, a mental programming. What that program consists of can either be negative in nature, or positive in nature.

When we are unaware of the paradigm, then that's when it determines the results we get, and the frustration begins because you consciously want one thing and your results show something else. The good news is that paradigms can be changed so that they are programmed with the results you actually want.

When you learn about how you get the results you want, it places you in the driver's seat and you can begin to steer your life in the direction you want to go. You will notice that the right people, situations and circumstances seem to automatically flow into your life, carving out the path of least resistance to push you towards your desired end results, your audacious goal.

HABITS

In this section we dove deeper into how those paradigms operate through our habitual patterns. Some habits are productive while others are non-productive. You can identify the non-productive habits by the results they yield. Are they bringing you closer towards your goal or are they pushing you away from it?

The problem most people make when working on their habits is tackling too many at once. I always recommend to my clients that they work on one or two habits at a time, this disrupts and weakens the paradigm that it's connected to, and it doesn't overwhelm you at the same time. If the habit is not in alignment with what you want or who you want to be, then rest assured its non-productive and more than likely connected to a negative paradigm you have running in your subconscious mind.

Often, these non-productive habits are the paradigm's way of staying active and preventing you from changing it. It's a survival tactic our subconscious mind uses through our actions to remain on course with its current programming. Again, these can be changed but first, you need to be aware of them and see them for what they really are; they are a set program running in your subconscious mind.

When you consciously begin to create new productive habits or start to reinforce existing productive habits, you are creating new neural pathways and associations within the brain. These send different signals to the body, creating different behaviors and actions. After doing this consciously for awhile, the new habits begin to happen automatically without you even putting effort into them. This is when you know that the subconscious mind has absorbed the information as a new positive paradigm, because your behavior has changed. Now, your actions will be producing different results and you're well on your way to achieving your goal.

FEAR

What an interesting, yet very powerful emotion. Fear can either completely debilitate you, or it can drive you to accomplishing great things in life. I went over with you that there is a difference between physical danger fear, and the fear that comes with change. When you begin to focus on the latter and see fear for what it really is, 'False Environment Appearing Real,' it puts you back into control.

Fear is a sign of growth and a shifting of existing, negative paradigms. Your old self-defeating paradigm will put thoughts into your conscious mind that tell you you're not smart enough, not likeable enough, not good enough. The main objective around this is to keep you where you are because you have developed programming over the years that is easy to follow and that is familiar. There is less danger and less risk in the familiar. But when you give into that fear and remain where you are, you're essentially imprisoning yourself with a life sentence of repeating the same unwanted results over and over.

I have come to the point in my life now that if something doesn't scare me on some level, I know there is no growth in it for me and I'm probably not aiming high enough. I use that fear emotion as a notification system that tells me that it's something that contains growth. The big one for me was speaking in public, which I know is a big one for many people. I read somewhere once that people would rather die, than to have to speak in front of others. How insane is that? But, that's how powerful your paradigm can be in talking you out of changing.

If your audacious goal scares you, good! That means it's 100% something you should be doing. That is your notification telling you that you're on the right track. When I retired from massage therapy, I was on a self discovery journey, so I worked in a corporate job for six years to figure out what I wanted. Leaving that corporate salary job to go back into entrepreneurship was scary as hell, but it is what I wanted to do and because I was studying this material and practicing it every day, I knew I was on the right track. It was by far the best thing I ever did because here I am now, writing this information to you.

Use that fear as your notification system for growth and know that on the other side of that fear is liberation and success.

SELF-IMAGE

What is the you who has already accomplished their goal doing right now? What does this future you look like? What does this future you feel and act like? When you tap into this, you are looking at the better parts of you that you want to really bring to the surface and to embody. You are identifying aspects of someone who is successful, kind, motivated and who looks for the best in others and in every situation they encounter.

There is a theme that you have probably noticed me go over several times now that says the 'you' that has already accomplished your set goal, is not the you that you are now. Have you ever thought about what you might say to a younger, less experienced version of yourself who might be frightened to do something they have never done before? Sit back and tap into who the you that has accomplished your goal already, and what advice does that "goal achieved you" have for the "present day you?"

The part of yourself that can achieve and succeed at any goal you set out to do, has some fantastic advice for the current you. When you hear the saying "you have all the answers inside of you," I personally believe that's what that means. Really, if you can think it up in your mind and you can picture yourself having reached that goal without worrying about all the 'how' aspects in-between, its more than accomplishable for you to reach.

Start thinking about who that future you is and start pretending that you are already that person. Doing this shifts your energies and changes your paradigm so quickly, because it's a non-identification to where you currently are with yourself right now. Remember, your subconscious mind doesn't know the difference between what is real and what is imagined. That self empowered, goal achieving, successful entrepreneur future you, is not in alignment with your current negative paradigm. So, bring that future you to the surface and act as if it's already happening.

NICHE & IDEAL CLIENT

Yes, you absolutely have the power of choice as to who you work with and who you are serving. Attracting people to you that are in alignment with your business and your goals is an amazing way to propel you even more into the success you are born to embody. Focusing on serving clients that are a match to your area of interest, will create so much business for you because you now have a focused niche.

Your niche is not your modality, so understand the difference between the two as it will save you a lot of headaches when creating your business plan.

When you spread yourself too thin and become a Jack or Jill of all trades, you never really become focused and you will be presented with anyone and everyone. It's similar to a treat bag you get at a birthday party; it's exciting, but you don't really know if you're going to like what you get or not.

Be clear about the type of clients you want that you enjoy working with, and that are going to help you specialize even more on a specific area. Figure out what problem you can solve for others and go looking for those clients, as they're also looking for you. You must first learn how your ideal client describes their problem and desired outcome in THEIR own words, as this will help you connect with them on a much deeper level.

If you do this, your new business is going to take off in no time!

SUCCESS THROUGH SERVICE

The energy of giving to others is unmatched by any other. When I talk about giving, I am speaking of leaving other people with the experience of increase, leaving someone with more than what they came with into an encounter with you.

When you go into a situation with a lack mindset, then you attract more lack. When you go into a situation with an abundance mindset, you attract more abundance. Like attracts like, and this couldn't be any truer than in this specific topic. You always hear "treat others how you would like to be treated." The reason this saying exists is because it's absolutely true.

Even though we cannot see it with our physical eyes, we are all energy and we are all emitting a frequency. Have you ever walked into a room and you could just feel the tension? Or you saw a friend or family member and just knew they were in a negative mood? This is all energy, and that energy comes back to you in equal proportions to what you give out.

When you go into any business with a fear mindset that involves competition, you are going to get a lot of competition. Your subconscious mind is going to look for situations to place you in that validates that mental programming you have. You will create for yourself an unnecessary struggle which will more than likely leak over to your bottom line.

Go into your business with the purpose to be of service to others and be grateful for that opportunity to do so. When you practice this art of leaving others with the experience of increase and have the success mindset in all areas of your business, you will find that exactly the right people and situations will magically attract themselves to you, like a moth to a flame.

POWER OF THE MASTERMIND

There is something to be said about the power of learning and working in groups. When you have multiple like-minded individuals coming together for a similar goal or purpose, magical things begin to happen. You come up with ideas and insights that, more than likely, you would not have come up with on your own.

I highly recommend you assemble a group of this nature and that you employ the Mastermind Principle in your own career. You will find your results will quantify themselves more than if you were to just figure things out on your own. Not only are you getting a direct download from others who have more than likely gone through and learned from an experience you're up against, but you can also do this for others in the group.

Every single one of us has our own experiences and perceptions about business and the obstacles we often encounter, and I can honestly say that without the support and assistance of my own mastermind group, I would not be where I am today in my own business.

> *"Success is nothing more than a few simple disciplines,*
> *practiced every day."*
> Jim Rohn

FINAL WORDS OF ENCOURAGEMENT

You are reading this book for a reason because if you weren't meant to, you would never have picked it up in the first place. I know that you have your fears and doubts, I did as well. But, if you trust and believe in yourself, and employ the suggestions I give to you in this book, you are going to find your career and life in general changing in wonderful ways.

The biggest and best investment you can ever make is the one on your own personal and professional growth and development. It's a skill you can transfer over to those you love and care about, and that you can use in any area of your life.

I want you to stop letting your old negative paradigms you have about success to determine the direction you go in life, and what you accomplish. You ARE in control and you ARE the director of your successes.

Follow your dreams, follow your passions and above all, follow your heart. Keep understanding yourself through studying mindset and moving forward towards your goals, and I promise you that it will happen much quicker than you ever imagined.

Move confidently in the direction of your dreams.

Good luck my friend.

Richard J. Platt

About the Author

Richard J Platt is a Massage Therapist since 2002 and a Certified Clinical Hypnotherapist since 2006, who studied in Canada and Germany. Richard now dedicates himself full time as a Business Success Coach for the massage therapy industry and is known for his online digital business coaching programs, *Massage Therapist Success Fundamentals and Niche Discovery Bootcamp.*

Through his advanced studies of the human mind, and his successful entrepreneurial experience of working both physically and mentally with clients for over 18 years, Richard utilizes his depth of knowledge to help his current students break through the many roadblocks that might be preventing them from creating success within their massage careers.

Richard has been privileged to have previously been trained and mentored under one of the world's leaders in human growth and potential, Bob Proctor, who starred in the hit movie documentaries *The Secret (2006) & Think and Grow Rich – The legacy (2017)*.

Richard now focuses his time solely on coaching massage therapists and other body workers in bridging the gap between what they truly want in their careers and the achievement of it. He does this through progressively moving them toward clear articulation of their own audacious, exciting goals. Richard helps his students realize and create the careers they want to have, by showing them how to get out of their own way.

Richard's time is dedicated to the growth of his online professional development coaching business, and currently lives on the west coast of Canada, in beautiful Vancouver, British Columbia.

Thank You!

Get Your Free Goal Setting Lesson Video!!

I wanted to thank you for reading *Massage Therapist Success Mindset – Success Principles for the Massage Therapist Entrepreneur*.

I'm excited to share with you my passion for this material, which was taught to me by some of the most successful thought leaders in the world— and I'm sincerely hoping some of it gave you the inspiration to do more!

My goal for you is to shift your perception and your way of thinking so that you can incorporate these new awareness's into your everyday routines so you can start seeing some speedy results. Reading this material is a great start. However, I've discovered that the easiest way to really absorb this information is to act on the lessons in this book and immerse yourself into these studies right away.

To get you started and as my gift to you, I'm giving you a **free goal setting lesson video** where I share some of my pro tips used by the industry's best, just for reading my book.

This lesson video is filled with great information which reinforces what you learned in the book, and gets you started on forming that clear goal and understanding your "why."

To receive your free video and worksheet, visit *richadjplatt.com/gift* and then let me know what action steps you're going to take from what you learned.

Email me at hello@richardjplatt.com

Happy Creating!
Richard J. Platt

"Goals are like magnets. They'll attract the things that make them come true."

Tony Robbins

Website: www.richardjplatt.com

CPSIA information can be obtained
at www.ICGtesting.com
Printed in the USA
JSHW031426180820
7365JS00003B/117